Also by Douglas Evan Weiss

Killer Mario Cuomo (with Asha Agnish)
Junglehead (with Asha Agnish)
Cobras And Caviar
Surfhead

Lightning Bolts And **Disco Girls**

DOUGLAS EVAN WEISS

Copyright © 2015 by 33 Orange Street

All rights reserved. No part of this publication may be reproduced, distributed, or transmitted in any form or by any means, including photocopying, recording, or other electronic or mechanical methods, without the prior written permission of the author, except in the case of brief quotations embodied in critical reviews and certain other noncommercial uses permitted by copyright law.

Printed in the United States of America at McNally Jackson Books, 52 Prince Street, New York, NY 10012.

Front and Back cover : Krystian Stjerne
Graphic design : Pauline Pérol

First Edition

For my friends and family and teachers,
with gratitude.

Goodbye Mama and Papa
Goodbye Jack and Jill
The grass ain't greener
The wine ain't sweeter
Either side of the hill.

-THE GRATEFUL DEAD

Resist much. Obey little.

-WALT WHITMAN

Lightning Bolts And **Disco Girls**

★ Part *one*

S A N D

*

PROLOGUE

what's a stringer? she asks. how do you get to Hollywood?
it's a busy night, all the tables are full, all the candles are lit. light jazz from the PA system, a constant hum of chatter and dishware. all the couples are trim, tan, handsome – play on their smart phones, a necessary reprieve. the boys talk ocean, drink wine, beer and soda – all their money obediantly spent on food and alcohol.

late mornings at the beach, evenings at the clubs. the girls so pretty, so rich; marching through the most recent inheritance, up from the streets, into the salty air, and breezy nights.

he paddled right past me and sat up at the point, Einstein says. so I turned to him and said 'hey friend – don't think you are going to sit up here and just take the next wave.'
and he started screaming, and saying 'what's your problem?'
so i says 'no problem bro, but I've been sitting here, waiting for a wave, and you just paddle right past me. not cool brother.'
then he says 'well, I'm from Hawaii!'

So I says 'bro, if you'd tried that in Hawaii, they'd have knocked your damn head off!'

before 6am no one is awake. the grounds are still, with only the sound of leaves rustling and ocean waves closely breaking. in the main house all the lights are off, except for a lone bright kitchen light shining. the doors are all shut, and the night watchman sleeps outside on a short two person wicker couch. the ground is warm, the air is heavy.

I watched him take a wave, Einstein says. he was shakey on a short ride. then I took the next wave, and paddled back up to the point, and say, 'man, I hope you shred it in Hawaii, because you just totally kooked that wave out here.'

the couples grope in the corner. they have holstered their gadgets for punk affections. he moves around to sit closer to her, and she reaches her arms around his neck, pulls him in closer, and kisses his round face fully.
she recedes gently and smiles, her hair long, past her shoulders, light brown, well placed, battling the heat.
Just for tonight, he tells her.
Just for always she replies.

beauty is always beauty – just that.
her skin is covered in ink; a tattoo the long length of her back, fully detailed, perfect; a dragon, an ocean beast, rising from the crashing waves, violently breaking the rough surface of a tumultuous sea, with fire wild and darkness looming across the horizon. a red beating sun, a flower and a serpent twisted in the love – the duality, the rebellion, the salty marriage.
same same, she kindly whispers, laughs, and lifts her red wine glass by the stem, glares into her lovers aging feminine eyes, and sings of disgust and grime and poverty and beauty and strength.

here we are again, she says. that's all there is.

The tattooed lady rests her hand on her lovers knee, and her lover spreads her hand over the tattooed ladies fingers, and digs her manicured red nails into her tan skin. lightly at first, then deep, heavy, accute.

her look conveys victory.

you have me here, her look says. across all the oceans and latitutes, into the heat and filth and lights. the foreign voices and unfamiliar languages, roasting in salt water and expectation.

look at my breasts, she thinks. they are fabulous, and you want to love all of me, endlessly, all night, unapoligeticaly, full of decipt and merry lust.

they lean in closer to each other, to hear the dirty whispers, the tease, the spit.

come to my place, the tattooed lady tells her curvaceous lover. it's empty, ready. no garbage, no fear.

no expectations, no problems.

SAND

obese, bursting, with spirit, hungry in rage, beautiful in life; just in town for a week, lets catch up.

drowning in women and water - the leisure class example of poverty and perversity - another round for the Russian girls and their frigid proclivities.

don't answer back to fast, don't lose sight of the shore. the older girls get all the looks, the saints are up in the back booths painting pictures and comparing rhymes. the white women (now you're courageous) feign peasantry and aloofness, glance at love and fortune, then heroically retreat to song and dance, parading across the beach, elevated to sand and spit. the dining room empties, the tycoons race back to the internet.

we did it for freedom! Einstein says. shirtless, in the early afternoon sun, fresh from another unseasonal rain storm, leaning against a concrete pillar, outside a crumbling corner house (now a factory), worn and exasperated, looking to The Gods for reason, over it all.

it was about the freedom! Einstein wails again. we did it because no one else wanted to, because not everyone could. so we went out there and destroyed ourselves to be like them - our rebellious heroes, our water God - but now everyone just wants to be seen......

Einstein rolls another cigarette at the small, round, yellow plastic two person table in the empty living room. random pieces of faded paper, coupons and loose tobacco are scattered across the dulled silver surface. wrinkled, alive, fuming, thoroughly dismayed and constantly fighting.

now we all line up, like a conveyor belt, like a line of mercenaries. a cookie cutter heap of short haired Aryans and their water sticks. 'ready for service, sir!'

he raises his hand to his forehead, simulating a serious salute, practiced in sarcasm and sorrow, pleading with his soft blue eye.

Is this what we've come to? he wonders aloud. is this the definition of you? us? them?

he steps back. a James Brown slide, a Leon Russell two step, and lights his smoke.

what the fuck! Einstein screams. Exasperated.

its about us, not you, he triumphantly concludes.

the wind continues to howl. less, less, less! she screams. fully into it, bending, complete, dancing between aware and functionality; oblivious and lost. seated, cross legged, humming: AUM.....! here we are, there we go.

glowing, radiant, colorful, the passing guards, the freedom, every moment the dream, every day the heroic arch. riding along the thin back roads, awash in spirit, the green mess, the breaking intrigue (the touch, a vein along the leafs delicate spine, the sun through the clouds). good morning concrete, good morning dirt. good morning sand, good morning water.

breath, Ganesh orders. first this pose, then that.

she stands in front of the crowd, enlightened, shining in speech and action.

we've all come here, Ganesh continues. we are all right here. there is no place else, there is nothing else. just now, simple. all the ancient figures descend, sit next to you, imagine the end, fused perfectly with the beginning.

just breath, she says. just do that, now, she orders.

surely she will destroy you (a day in the life).

she appears - a surprise, a promise - and sprays the wafting scent of wild and scattered time. boiling passions (sit still for just a few moments), while the assaults occur: pheromones, sex, pain, bliss, bewilderment, obsession; this tiny puncture, this beautiful place, this paradise, with the mad men and the fearless women and the rebel children - playing exact, unbound, in love - self and others – equal, exotic, strange and aloof, the great train robbery, the grand escape.

here and everywhere, the magnificent pulse, the great caring endeavor; the redwood eyes, the dark olive skin, the lost laughter and vintage indecision – the young girls and the lead road, the globe and the endless sea; the deck, the sail and the wood; the proximolicom wondering and blind ambitious commitments to service, action and verse; taking off deeper, being smarter, grateful and infinite, with endless potential and immaculate heartbreak.

wet is the atom, snapping is the sinking E chord.

delicious angels and tough stamped men portray the greatest of mystic actions and lifted dedications, to the bending tree and hungry sun.

hungry hungry hungry.

there are so many things i could do, she laments. just have to pick one......

they arrive lost and lonely, searching for love, freedom and happiness. they arrive upon steel ships and ingest the salt water, the wind and the sun; and are gone.

they disappear, dance across the cliffs, drown in the sand, fly across the waves, die under the stars. a full invitation, a timeless smile, healthy in hot water, mired in grief, burning, the easy music and quiet cafes, the blue and grey hues of sky, cloud and business.

defeated by plastics, indiscriminate in sex and bathing, kisses and milk, prayer and devotion – here till the oceans rise, high as the great city towers, with rogue wave derelicts of days past. the giant heroic faces and quiet demeanor, across North Africa and Mongolia and Europe, focused and divine, rebellious and beautiful; one hand on the elephant and the other on the whip. forward, forever, for her, and broken and war.

hati hati, fun fun – everyone is just looking for a good time........
the catwalk: let it all go, let there be love.

all chill, all mellow, just watch it rise and fall, the beast at the banquet, the ginger girl on top; the eternal thug poets, seaside gangsters, and witty endeavors – around the chin, dazzled and poor, groovy and spinning; tonight and tomorrow, forever and radical.

can we simplify the love and sex and just do it all till its time to leave? she plainly asks.

enough with the guilt, enough with the ruckus. stomp out the noise, again we be here, rugged in scripture, peaceful in premise, along the sides of the cliffs, up and down the Peninsula, clean and mighty – just paint me something colorful and special, just imagine those eyes around your soul.

enough with the romance! Brussel Sprout wails. get inside of me and lets have some fun!

live like a raptor, ready to go with death.

don't take all day, i've got to be back at the beauty salon in thirty minutes, she tells Henry.

the whole world stares and waits. the wobbling celebratory drunk party queen, the strutting kings. through great dedication and sustained commitments, make it about us (all of us) and allow that marvelous soaring beauty, expands and grows.

simply be. all of us, we just are..... Ganesh hints.

if i had a hammer, i'd hammer in the morning, i'd hammer in the evening, all over this land....

the sunshine and red flower walkways, up and down the great path. the heroes walk easily, with acceptance, honest, permanent, till the body withers and falters, till the sport continues to trend, till the lights go out. and with a twist, a mantra, a whiff of gratitude, the lactic star dust atmosphere divine spreads, with the wailing colors and electric guitars; with the roller coaster lifestyle and the dollar fifty dinners; with the open air temple and the wet pulpit; with the crazy Germans and the nervous Canadians; with the wild simple Australians; with the flat tails and art deco reputations.

play the funk! Ganesh orders. start up the boat, set up the

drums, bring in the ocean; we are all going to the show, we are kissing all the girls!

not sure what city we are in, she adds. not sure which island is up. but the water is warm, and the noodles taste good.

get comfortable, Ganesh orders. the fire works are about to begin.

Brussel Sprout sits down, tall and pretty, all in black, with her breasts bumping out of her faded black cheap cotton tang top shirt. hand made jewelry hangs uneven from her ears and wrapped around her thin wrists. this is it, the end, the hatchet, the gallows; goodbye child, hello woman – its happening.

how have you been? Brussel Sprout asks, then interrupts to tell where she has traveled over the past months.

did you miss me? she asks. of course you did, you must have. i'm a dream, i'm a wrecking ball. aren't you glad to have me back in your life? aren't you glad its not over......

the wind picks up a bit in the afternoon, and the air is cool, as the sun edges towards an endless blue horizon. a golden glow, her milky skin and hard butter lips.

just be good, she tells him directly. then exits to another mans house.

at the beach its busy, with cafes full and young sun burnt children running around with plastic. the late afternoon stretches out and yawns – its a mad house, a paradise, a pit stop, a Treme marching band. the aches, the ongoing march to water, the metaphysical retreat plan.

her t shirt reads "with great power comes great responsibility".

she takes off her top and lays back in the sand. her back slightly arched to fit the contours of the beach. eyes closed, legs long and strong, muscles hard around the thighs and tight at the knees.

we are here forever, Brussel Sprout moans.

the sun bakes her.

i hope to burn up, she says.

SAND

come back to my house, Henry says directly.

its one in the afternoon, she says absently. to early for all that rolling around.

you kill me, he says.

he turns his head and looks down the beach at all the other women, in thin bikinis and big sunglasses, and he wonders how he came to be sitting here, with this butterfly, who wont make love to him in the afternoon.

if you are bored then go surfing, she instructs.

its too hot, he tells her.

so now you understand, she finalizes.

the water is colder then usual.

Henry wades in up to his knees, and feels the hard reef under his bare feet, and the cool water wash up his skin - the chill and the calling. he paddles out and watches the waves break, machine like, on to the reef. the energy hits and rises up and breaks over itself, consuming..... a wave, a roller coaster, a toy, an adventure. a mad, lust full obsession.

i wonder if she is watching? he thinks.

its a bubble, its a bubble - we are all friends, in the bubble.....

its a bubble, and we are all friends in the fucking bubble, he says clearly.

clean as acid rain, when the party ends and all the people parade past, into the gravel parking lot on a hill, with corn vendors and transport drivers, fully armed and ready to go. the full sweep of drunk and random promiscuity, burning with risky flavors and dirty dreams.

all the motherfuckers, Ganesh spits.

she watches them pass, elegant and shanty. all with a tattered air of fabulous and heartbreak. drunk on salt and air, mixing the flavors, again.

i'm a motherfucker, Brussel Sprout says.

light and versatile, direct and simple in fashion. her dark purple hoody sweatshirt casually hangs below her hips. tight black spandex pants cut slightly short above the ankles. the body, the grace.

next time you have a party you invite me, Ganesh demands. we bring the funk and the fuck! she says victoriously.

you can come over anytime, Leopold tells her. put on some music, have some tea, relax. anytime.....

yes, Ganesh celebrates. the good funk.

yes, the good funk, Larry Levan says.

Ganesh smiles and nods her head. its late yet the party continues to let out. strangers, con artists, whores and hustlers. all the beautiful Gods. all the local brass bands.

they are all so pretty, Brussel Sprout says, watching the procession pass in front of them.

maybe all enlightened, Larry Levan continues, enjoying the intellect and the sound of his voice.

i know you love me, Larry Levan tells a gang of Brazilian girls that pass by. maybe not tonight, but another time. surely.

i love you, one girl courageously answers.

sometimes yes, another adds. sometimes no.

you simple beast, you allusive angel. certainly its a dream, a jump shot, a methadone clinic, a Misfit Tour stop. first in, last out, hati hati, its a spiritual thang.......

Mr Heavy walks in the front door with four Asian hookers and asks for a table. the manager knowingly smiles. with a sweep of his left hand he orders an empty round table in the corner of the dimly lit open air dining room to be set and prepared.

a young boy rushes over and places a candle and five emerald green cloth napkins on the table. he wipes the varnished dark wooden chairs with a dry rag that hangs from his hip, then disappears into the kitchen. shows over.

they sit, and the girls continue to giggle. all dressed in black, with short spandex mini skirts (all of them) and ostentatious colorful high heal shoes. pinks, baby blues, teals and beige. one wears a thin orange scarf around her neck.

a bottle of red wine and two pizzas, Mr Heavy orders. vegetarians, he amicably barks at the squinting manager. and send over five spoons please, he adds, as the manager loosely walks away.

feel that motherfucking bass in your face, feel that motherfucking bass in your face.....

the dirt and grime gone clean. the modern rebel sound track. its a new year, a progressive form, a silent diatribe; a love scene, a release.

what comes next? The Gods wonder. we've had the retro, the aggression, the influx, the short revolution, the progression movement, the airel assault, the riots. the girls and the social media secrets revealed. the name brands and the hipster happiness executions. the raw vegan diet and the Mexican mariachi beach music.

we have had the celebrities, the glossy magazines, the monthly zines, the books sold out the back of the car on the way to Trestles. the large money contracts, the animals, the Euros, the globalization of foam and fun. the middle finger and Jimi Hendrix passing by. we've had the toxins, the spills, the acid and the advertisements. Jock Sutherland and Brad Gerlach. the groupies and the accountants.

and now what? Einstein asks.

a thick heavy bass line, The Gods reply. a wild ride, a perfect gun, a quiet revolt (don't tell anyone, its happening now). an electric sample, one giant fin, a constant smile and a shrug – redefining the traditional idea of handsome, holds the door open every time, slides down the rainbow and takes off deep – cruisy, mellow arched way back – all that soul, all that karma burning off.

its the glorious time of the compassionate beast, The Gods continue. the sex stance, the one night shrug around here. the city, the jungle, the flat tummy, the red dress, the last drop of poison. slowly, gliding across the face, buried in the sand.

Lightning Bolts and Disco Girls

how can you not want to go to the beach? Einstein asks.

impregnated with optimism and stoke (its so rad, its so awesome – we are all so cool.....), island revolutions, less is more, mellow is beautiful, quiet is God, all are One.

small wave infatuations, anonymous glory and boundless courage. Einstein hears it all.

all are one.

if you will suck my soul then i will eat your funky emotion.

in the early morning haze there is a massive paddle out, a new age dawning. the best time ever.

turn up the bass, bring down the treble, get wet, be fabulous, burn the fancy, smile and believe. my haute couture sweetheart, my dirty bungalow on the beach.

maybe if we all loved each other a little more? The Gods wonder.

maybe if it were about finding the peace, Ganesh replies.

here is the revolution, still going. all ballsy, free, expressive and exciting. go hard or fuck off, the t-shirts all read.

hard and happy, dressed in black, with a little red flavor. a string around the neck, a jet plane around back; a dollar bill and a flame thrower. you motherfucker, you legitimate beauty; all in and desperate, fleeting, now smile, she loves you greatly.

talk to me.....talk to me......

a butterfly sits on the edge of a cliff, over looking the sea, with a flower in her hair, and laments her impending departure.

I am so sad, Magdelena says. i'm counting away the hours. last night was the worst night ever...... i just sat and watched the clock, and now i am so sad, because i must go.

she fixes her hair, sits nearly naked in the sun, and watches the waves pour in. the swell is picking up now. in her sorrowful beauty, drowning in dreams of somewhere else, transfixed in here, running, because that is what they do, they run.

i had a nice night with Leopold, Magdelena says. but i could not stay there. always my mind jumps to where i am going, never where i am. today the island, tomorrow Kuala Lumpur..... Qatar, Europe, then who knows. a gorgeous mess, an unforgiving clock.

he loves me, and i love him, she says. but its useless. its a dream, and i am slowly waking up.

she has a strong walk, yet elegant. holding all that sex and vile; dangerous and fleeting.

watch me, Magdelena says. this is life, don't worry about anything. in the morning i'll be gone. gone and gone and gone. and you will have my walk in your head, and you will remember all the things we did not do.

broken, with the revolving morning air and the ludicrous march of time; wild, free of yearning, watch this gait, drown in this honey. she leans in, rests her bare elbow on a knee high stone wall, twists around, and breathes.

i am fabulous, Magdelena says. marvelous, milky, and tight. the apex of young lust and road weary delights. the hitchhiker, the groupie, the butterfly, the sand. i am a jet plane, a singing drop of rain; the sharpened tip on the horns of a rampaging bull. i am sheer beauty, a glowing flower, a spot of color on a dark horizon.

come here and try to kiss me, she orders. come here, longing for touch, peace, and reprise. it don't cost a thing, but it aint cheap; my gypsy love affair, my spiral surge; my tranie ways, my rock and roll walk.

i am your dream, your morning wet dream, your full time tramp. away with the talk, come over here so we can fuck.

Brussel Sprout has difficulty getting into her shorts. cut off blue jeans, tiny, with a large square leopard skin patch on the left front leg. she heaves and shimmies, finally able to pull the faded waist band above her protruding hips. she gives the shorts one last pull, jumps up off the ground, and slides all the way in, twisting and dry.

short, the cuffs arrive way above the thighs, and curve upwards into her hard round buttocks. tattooed, worn, with the miles well represented by her outfit: a yellow wife beater shirt slipped over her black bikini top. the scent of salt water and sex, still pungent on her skin, across her lips, as she smiles, stretches out in the sun, and prepares to leave again.

you are fun, Brussel Sprout tells him. you are a distraction. but now i must go. do not think about me much. do not wait for me to come back. this is what you wanted, she says. this is all you can handle.

the waves crash heavy now at the bottom of the cliff line. the air turns warmer and the breeze dies out. couples make plans.

its all about the love.......

life is one giant text message, Leopold concludes to Ganesh, under a coconut tree on the south end of the beach.

its not about you, its about us, Einstein repeats to himself, in a color filled room, alone and working.

Peter Pan got beat up last night, now everybody is out for blood. its a death march, a sinuous circus, a paddle ball game. with the ferocity and the beautiful sunsets. all in, all happening.

his face wasn't as bad as everyone thought it would be. a swollen right cheek, puffed up below his handsome jaw line and dark full beard. he looked like he'd been stung by a wasp, instead of a roundhouse kick by a stranger.

its getting out of hand! Mr Heavy says loudly, pacing around a sparse living room in the early morning. the sun is lightly shining through the open doors, the simple plastic white shades rattle gently in the breeze.

Mr Heavy has been awake all night, going on two days now, and his thin body is beginning to reveal the bender. from this beach to the next, this club to the next, this island to that one.

he finally sits in an armless wooden chair, in his signature tight black jeans, shirtless, sweating.

its just getting out of hand, he laments again. all these fights, in and out of the water. everybody walking around angry and gruesome all the time.

its just madness! he concludes.

the boys agree. they nod their heads, sink further into the black leather sofas.

we didn't come here for this, he continues. fuck, i like it here plenty, and want to have my children here, my family here – its my home!

he twists his face and looks up at the boys.

you know what i mean? he pleads.

we know, the boys mumble in unison, and nod, and drink from their half empty cans of beer.

they reluctantly agree to do whatever it takes. to parade down the boulevards, if necessary, and confront the assailants, the terrorists, and tenants.

we must call everyone together, Mr Heavy resounds. a meeting of all the heavy dudes, and sort out what is going on around here. and i want ideas from everyone! whatever you think, whatever it takes, to get this place back to amicability, beauty, peace and understanding.

there is a pause. the sun is shinning brightly. there is a gentle hum from the passing traffic along the main road.

i love you guys, Mr Heavy concludes. it should not be like this.

Brussel Sprout rampages in, hectic and beautiful, with the universe swirling around her. spacey, above it all, 3 feet off the ground, always excited, with a million lovers and no real friends.

i have three choices where to live, Brussel Sprout says to Henry. i can go live with Darwin, and become a drug addict. i can live in a house with four alcoholics and get deported. or i can rent a villa for more money then i have and go completely broke.

she turns on her white smartphone and scrolls through her messages. stern faced and adamant about everything. her dark brown hair falls below her silky shoulders. her light coffee colored skin, her youthful ambivalent face. her endless body, voluptuous, tempting, used, heartless, constantly desired.

busy busy now.

she is only supposed to be in town for a few days. connecting, networking, searching. somewhere between peace and asshole. the travesty, the aging hippies, the phosphorescent pin up girls; kind smiles and flirtatious winks. whatever you want, where ever we are. surrounded by the strange, the magic, the voodoo – here we are, sitting across from the young starlets, with nothing to say.

we could be here forever, she says to Henry, with a thin smile.

if nothing comes through for me in America, or no boats are leaving for Cape Town, then this might be home again, she concludes with a sigh. you may be stuck with me, friend.

a friend? Henry recoils.

i had hoped so, she confidently states.

Up in the morning, out on the job/work like the devil, for my pay.......

The early morning, the dry reef, at first sunlight, all her majestic ocean, calm, naked, just up, with a touch of light, a handful of peace. The poets all read about heroism, about grit, about giving something up, to capture an allusive courage, to build self discipline; to become the beast, the savant, the allusive guy leaning against the wall in a shady corner. The thick warm air, already, an urban jungle boom, newly minted, foiled, with a taste of concave, soap and love – loose and wild at all the celebrity functions, unknown and stiff with the secretaries and bean counters. All beautiful, again. All burning, somewhere.

forget safety
live where you fear to live
destroy your reputation
be notorious.

Rumi, graffitied on all the bathroom walls.

you perfect whore, you gypsy motherfucker...... again to the left, again asking for love and pussy. 3 feet deep and treacherous

SAND

- tell us stories about the city, tell us lies about the island. 5 miles out, 5 years back (it's always 5 years, it's always a tittle fight).

pick me up on the way there, you sexy half moon, you notorious Jew, you switchblade devil - it cuts, it burns; it looks like a Ferrari, it sounds like Don Rickles.

pay me up front, let the water follow me all the way out. sama sama in gold, jalam jalam in red. waving at the shiny love affairs, swapping spit with the young Aussie girls, on a restless Saturday night in August - just hanging out, just passing time.....

come sit over here. you queen, you devil, you hypodermic needle. jalam jalam, from the backseat of a 57 Chevy, jungle green, puta soft, endlessly happy, gone...... power naps and old school hip hop, before the sandy hoes let loose and the serendipity boys demand another gig, another chance, another pimp starter kit, dripping in blue.

(dripping in blue).

when the band kicks in and the hardcore starts, for the wayward angels and Bucktown alumnus.

the meadow, the Columbus Avenue, the sunflower seeds, the nickel bags, the tapes, the skyline, the blades and the colors; the grass and the bottles, the boxes (it never rained); the last verse, the photographs, the books, the chains, the hats; once here, once under the moon.

you knife, you wave, you motherfucker. The Gods are watching.

so sharp, so beautiful, so radical, with a zinger, with a bite at the lip - if these fingers dig into your hips, move you around, hold it down, try not to cum, and drink it all in - the heavy weight, the professional, the glory. how do i look in pink? all night long. all night long, on the dance floor, waiting for you to show up, as we boogie, as we dream.

I've been loving you........ the grand adventure, the long term game plan (everyday, everyday); fuck Hollywood, fuck the game. the young girls will kill you, the white girls just talk.

all the breath, all the freedom, all the love.

Lightning Bolts and Disco Girls

I am a motherfucker, Ganesh admits. I am a buffalo soldier.

fuck all the bullshit - it's a big pool of water with lots of people in here. sunshine mornings and grace. ahhhhh.

the bubble, the motherfucker......

I'm a mothefucker, Ganesh repeats. its the prevalent sentiment.

everyone is working. everyone is mad. a divine stop on the path, a special village, a last stop on the killing spree, a peaceful bastion; a rainbow, a place to love.

strange, Brussel Sprout says at the bottom of the stairs, watching all the faces pass by. waiting, breathing, semi patient.

we actually are living here, Henry, Brussel Sprout tells him. we are just us. with the heavy, with a smile.

hello lover, hello big time.

swirling, the affect of it all. the money tree, the dance music.
talk to me.......

heavy heavy, again. abating civility, groveling through a young middle age, beautiful in sight and penchant and catastrophe. bueno, with a tinge, with a pocket full of rainbows and a briefcase full of cash.

it's a bubble.

we are all in the motherfucking bubble, Ganesh says.

learning to be a motherfucker, learning how to break out of prison. a sash and a vision of some strange woman's cleavage. $20 for drinks and ice, enthralled with the old pictures of Padang, the legends, how we used to do it, how the single fins bring it all back; the same but different.

asphalt heartbreak and oceanside dreams leaves all the heavy gangster girls on the hook for penitence. blindly in love with them all, purposely fucking none of them, just to see what happens.

Henry plans accordingly.
if you will suck my soul.....

everyone sits down, communal style, at a long wooden table. friends, lovers (old and new), affairs, artists and business men;

girls and boys, straight and curvaceous, wallowing under the cut moon and cloudy night sky.

how long are you here for? Ganesh asks.

don't know, Brussel Sprout replies. how long are you here for? she asks.

don't know, Ganesh answers.

the drinks spill into the air, the food is hot and spicy - indigenous flavors, the long time gestures and slanted looks.

we can go anywhere, Brussel Sprout says. and Henry listens quietly, half ashamed, accepting.

you are a motherfucker, he says to himself. you know nothing. you are a speck, a star, a light year, a magnet and a friend.

there is noise. the hounding layers of people talking, the simple divine intellectualism, inspired by sand and water, from previous lives forgotten, and new homes found. its a fine place to write a novel, its a fine place to be a poet. turn up the music, listen to the wind, imagine Ginsberg, and congruent Melville infatuations. on the edge of the slow moving blade, on the way up to fabulous, on the end of a drumstick.

she slides in, nonchalant, busy, spinning, young, without expectations, without sin - and everyone looks up, and views her as kind and sincere, piercing (those almond eyes, that melancholy walk - all for the bubble, all for the chocolate).

we are just here to have fun, Henry tells her. forget your small worries, your petty concerns, your heavy arch. forget what you were supposed to know, what you were given and taught. this is what is supposed to happen. this is the greatest night ever. so let me kiss you, so let me be clear: this ain't about the cash - this is me dancing at midnight; this is Twelfth Avenue at sunset; something different, something forever.

make it till New Years Eve, fall off the edge of the world; this is where all the butterflies come, Henry tells her. just sit back and breath.

of course you love me, Brussel Sprout says to him. its the only thing you don't know how to do. yet we are doing it so so well.

work work work.....she is doing a thousand things.....

texting, she says with a mischievous smile. thats how it all starts.

she waves her hand in the air, flips a sarong around her neck, draped over her bare right shoulder, and dramatically walks into the grocery store. the lights on so bright and the streets so busy.

inside she flips through the fruits and vegetables, observing the miscellaneous colors, the patterns, the curves; she wanders through the aisles, searching for nothing, amongst all the boxes, the plastic packages, the colorful pictures and layered ingredients.

everything in here will kill you, she says to herself. everything in here is dying.

she peruses the soft drinks along one aisle, then the packaged soups along another, before circling back around and discovering the nuts and chocolate bars and oatmeal raisin cookies along the back wall. the height of civilization, the whole consumer paradigm, just awaiting inspiration, just digging a little walk under the hot florescent lights.

fifteen thousand miles for a better selection of dried noodles and exotic looking vegetables, she thinks to herself.

there is a hum through out the store, a monstrous AUM, a pervasive inner dialogue - everyone is doing it, everyone is disintegrating - on their smart phones, lost in the lights, pondering pasta, sexually ambivalent in the dream (maybe her, maybe her....), tattooed and out of petty cash, into the open air, with a persistent hatchet charm, with their knees behind their heads and a deep smile reminiscent of Christmas.

the wild tan skin girls...... she thinks to herself. that is what i'm a needing. she watches them pass, quickly paced along the white and black square linoleum floors, with a mysterious, lingering purpose that she cannot recall.

where are we all going? she thinks to herself.

what are we going to do with all this stuff? she whispers to herself, just loud enough to feel it, to make it real, to worry.

SAND

she is gnawing slightly, angry and desperate. For air, excitement, peace.

just breath, she says to herself, silently this time. this is not the place to fall in love, not the time to be lost, she tells herself.

she pays for a pack of peanuts and a tangerine, with crumpled dirty bills, small money, and she watches with wry humor as the cashier fumbles through the register drawer, while the cue grows and everyone sweats.

thanks for the good times, she compassionately tells the cashier.

thanks for the sunshine, she thinks.

walking out into the warm night air, weighted only by memory and dream, free for the headlight songbirds and the motorcycle savants. welcome back, she thinks. now go home and forget it all.

*

the street feels heavy, though the air is cool. a slight wind up the avenue, along the cascading streets, meeting on all the corners.

his boots are hard and strong along the concrete. against it, with it, stingingly at home.

Henry reminisces on all the buildings, all the landmarks, and all the shops.

this one is new, that one is surprisingly still here.

the garbage, the intimate smell, the elevating lights, the spinning wheels and running clocks. all the beautiful girls.....

he skips across Houston Street, straight down Broadway, takes a right onto Prince.

this feels the same but different, he thinks to himself. I've done this before. remember and pass, he tells himself. but its not the same, not really.

Henry pauses on the corner of Mercer Street and looks through

Lightning Bolts and Disco Girls

an open doorway into the bar and cafe area at the Mercer Hotel.

it's early, he thinks to himself. a late Monday morning.

a young thin Kansas looking boy with a short military style hair cut stands behind the bar and methodically dries a high ball glass with a clean white dish rag. the bar is small and vacant. across the room two of the four small round metallic tables are taken, each occupied by a single patron, devotedly dressed in black, both reading the New York Times.

a women – older, thin, beautiful – with a hard style and a chic history, flips through the Metro section. she sips her black coffee, slowly. her loose, tailored black sweater drops to her waist, meets a pair of tight black designer jeans. Converse sneakers, dark olive green, Varvatos design, are spotless and new. her black rimmed glasses are bulky, ugly, expensive.

she looks strangely familiar, he thinks to himself.

Henry stands in the doorway, smiles, and offers a sympathetic nod to the bartender, then continues to scan the room.

there is nothing for you here, he thinks to himself. its all been done. where is Guy Santochi? he wonders. where is Grand and Archibald?

a tinge of melancholy. a wiff of relief.

Prince Street is waking up. a fresh rush of delivery trucks and vacant taxi cabs. the cobblestones stretch under the weight of commerce and industry – benign, in fashion, bold and able. the crash of construction, the rush of progress, the magnetism of creativity.

Henry walks towards West Broadway, slowly. he skips off the curb and moves professionally between the constant traffic. he touches the taxi cabs and delivery trucks at the light. he continues down the crowding sidewalk, past the hair salons and Jim Morrison photograph galleries, until he finally reaches West Broadway.

he pensively pauses on the corner and looks up and down the small avenue. he decides to proceed south, into the downtown horizon, past all the mannequins, past all the pretty paint splattered canvases, neatly hung, sparsely economical, built for speed and fortune.

remember this? he thinks to himself. remember when you were rich and notorious. when these streets owned you, and you respected that obscene sense of slavery. when you were fully here, simple, without the wandering, without the doubtful pangs and inept tributes. the morning meetings, the late night girls, the all night promises. remember the walks along the Hudson River, the hunger and freedom; the restitution and frightening ambitions.

there is a continuous chill in the air, and Henry raises the colar on his old blue Hugo Boss sports jacket, digs his chin into his chest, and marches towards the river.

i think like a guy, Brussell Sprout says to him. she takes short sips from her bottle, choreographed perfectly.

Henry watches keenly, for the subtitles in her response. excited and bored, simultaneously.

at times, she says to him curtly. but it does depend.

thank God, Henry exclaims.

Sly had himself a water problem, and all the girls knew it. splash splash, the run down is simple: up the stairs, down the stairs, sama sama. wind blows and the sun peaks out from behind the noon day sky.

if she calls, Sly thinks, then i'll be funky all day. the best kid in Brooklyn, the uptown darling.

make this look good, he says to himself. just cutting greens and peeling potatoes. juice the kale and let the rock and roll sway away all the blues, all the wanton desires and passing fads.

the young lady digs into a green salad and pretends to be lady day with an organic addiction. makes all the boys smile. the coconut trees sing ' mama mama, mama mama....' just like the preacher said it would be, just like the music and the heartbreak.

a fan of the poison, guest of the dream, Sly thinks. simply

relive these kisses, and let the water do her thing.

Sly cries to the horizon and spends all of his mamas sweet wet coin on the kale juice and the hummus wraps. the American girls get famous and the yoga classes grow everyday.

spring me from this damn cell, Sly tells The Gods. i'm a bring back a case of sunshine and a little love for the urban homies.

Brussel Sprout digs into a veggie burrito, and snarls at his business ideas and daily infidelities.

love is a motherfucker, Sly tells her. don't believe that bullshit back talk and their petty admissions. if that fool loves you then he'll be back around before sunset with a box of chocolates and a chocker collar, bleeding from the teeth and dancing across the beach, just to get back here on time, with all that pirates wealth and Clooney charm – works on all the marvelous nomad women, sure as the rain gets you wet, and the gold makes you smile.

he might cut it with those two month visa backpack fuck fuck girls, Sly continues. but in this hood its hot and sharp, and it will cut you and leave that guru sunshine smile bleeding out on the uptown platform of the B train, if necessary. we are all simply dying on this God God island.

she takes another bite of hummus and knocks back a shot of vinegar, collects her keys and Baudelaire books, and walks down the four steps onto the sun drenched sand.

on the beach again, she goes and sits closer to Ganesh, away from the plans, the numbers, the macho heroes and slumbering princes.

don't call me no more! Ganesh is yelling at the clouds, the salt water and the frightened lovers. this bitch ain't got no time for your wiggle wiggle thump thump.

Sly takes out half a bar of wax and feels the earth rotate. all smooth, all groovy. he watches the Russian girl on the beach. fixates on a skinny brunette with a bold letter black tattoo that says 'HARD' across her flat tan stomach.

my last day, Cat Women says with a sigh.

been out with the drink and the boys? Sly asks.

yes, she replies softly. tired. bored. fucked.

and i leave tomorrow, Cat Women tells him, with patches of sand lightly caked on her cheeks and sun burnt nose.

we should have a good time today, Sly tells her, moving in closer, his voice low and confident.

she shrugs her shoulders and attempts a smile.

what are we to do? she asks, and buries her head in an American flag beach towel.

we could go back to my place, Sly tells her. or we could rent a room here, on the beach.

her smile hardens. the ocean crashes closer to her feet as the tide continues to rise, and Sly watches the clear blue water shimmer under the rising early afternoon sun.

the waves crash along the reef, courted by hungry surfers and their nomadic ways.

no, i cannot, she tells him with a smile. i am not that kind of girl.

Sly smiles at the rejection, assured of her temptation and fear, reveling in his own courage, fleeting and warm.

well, when you come back you give me a call, and we will get some cash and go out for some fun, he concludes.

Sly stands to leave and extends his hand in farewell. she puts her thin fingers into his, and daintily shakes his hand. Sly holds her hand for two seconds longer then she expects. she pulls away silently, and he obeys, and lets her go.

goodbye, Cat Women tells him.

goodbye Cat, he says with a smile, and saunters back up the beach and into Cafe Leon, where his dirty canvas bag and dry surfboard awaits him.

Einstein leans in and looks Henry straight in the eye. he smiles, slightly crooked, evenly stained in salt and decades and bone.

you hear me now, don't you? Einstein asks. because i worry. and that worry does no good unless we care, and i care a lot; so don't go out there being a hero, being a star all the time. just keep it mellow and bright, steady, with some damn style, so that when you go over the edge you know its all real. its all really happening.

time is a motherfucker, Einstein tells him.

she sings him a slow romantic French song that makes him dream in black and white, of older men and younger women, with ostentatious minks and big hats. he dreams of cigarette smoke rising into the night air, above the out door cafe tables, around the local Plaza, so far from him.

we have come to the other side of the world, Ganesh tells him. all this way, now what have you got to tell me? cough up some news! she hastily demands.

Sly thinks for a moment, flips through the weeks events: the bitter victories and tangible failures. what have i been doing? he thinks to himself.

a lovely French woman is arranging an orgy for us, Sly tells her. you should come.

she smiles, thin, perversely, interested.

not my style, Ganesh says. but you should call Cat Women. she loves that type of action.

of course she does...... Sly says,

he takes another long sip of carrot juice and feels the the universe open up a bit more.

no small talk, Sly tells her.

Ganesh finishes her whisky and soda and flags the waiter down to order another.

make it a bit stronger this time, she requests with a smile. all lips and daggers.

Cat is a legend, Ganesh tells Sly. complete party girl, total fuck machine.

perfect, Sly says. give her my number, my bank account and my gold. send photos and legal documentation. prove her age and my people will wire the cash.

SAND

they sit in silence for a short time. Ganesh stirs the ice cubes around her narrow highball glass, watches the amateur rock star girls at the nearby tales, with shaved heads and fading ambitions, waiting for trouble and local recognition, from the high paying boys and the main street Mafia girls in the tight black pants and designer sunglasses.

Sly watches the twist in Ganesh's neck, the young lines in her face, the tight muscles along her stone chin. he admires the dim curiosity in her eyes, and the glorious posture.

let all the little girls drown in that fading spotlight, Ganesh tells herself. the real men love me forever.

Sly watches the girls.

they would devour you, Ganesh tells Sly. you don't have the courage, you don't have the moxy.

Sly takes the punch like a man, absorbs the blow, breathes, fades, then comes back.

you have her try this urban concoction, Sly says with bravado. have her sample all the chocolate, cry all the colors, and watch the waters pass. then we can converse about appetites and ambitions. tell her its just you and I, Ganesh. a couple of pillows and a few metaphors.

she smiles, thin, and winks an eye.

come over here! he snaps at Ganesh. test me.

she slides out of her white wooden chair, comes around the table and sits closer to him. closer then he expected. she slides her hand along his leg, inside the thigh, over the shorts, and whispers in his ear.

this is all your gold, all your words, all your troubles. bite me until it hurts, and imagine that i came for you.

when you finally scream, then you will remember me forever, Sly tells her slowly.

this is forever, she laments.

Henry scrolls through the names in his phone.

social masturbation, he thinks to himself. none of them really

Lightning Bolts and Disco Girls

want to get naked, he thinks. better to save the cash and rest up for the swell.

Mr Heavy rides up like an explosion and orders red wine for the last two single girls, finishing their fettuccine, in the main room.

we gotta get some gunpowder and a few hookers and go down to the beach in style, Mr Heavy gallantly says.

Henry sends an ill faded text to Cat Women.

what are you doing? he texts. boring and slow.

quit peddling over them flimsy white girls, Mr Heavy orders. if we pop a few pills we can get to town on the back of this here storm, and be neck deep in pussy by midnight.

Henry sends another message.

lets just make love, he writes, desperate and scared.

tomorrow i am going to buy a Zodiac boat. get out to Padang quicker, Mr Heavy says.

he leans over the table, puts his hand on the lower back of a skinny Ukrainian girl at the next table.

what ya say honey? Mr Heavy whispers. you and me, just for a night, before the Armageddon begins.

she shrugs, and asks the waiter for another bottle of red.

just like a gypsy, Mr Heavy says. anything for a good time.

Henry's phone beeps.

Yes, it reads.

and then tomorrow we can drive north, Mr Heavy tells her. and you can bury me at the beach, with an eternal flame above my shallow sandy grave. just like the Bhagavad Gita predicts; just like all the good warriors predicted.

Henry takes the crumpled bills from his pocket and tries to pay for his tea.

nonsense! Mr Heavy yells. if this were the Titanic i'd be a fucking iceberg.

"and those who don't like the danger soon find something else to try....." he gallantly quotes.

SAND

she wants love and other disasters, Henry Castle says. but i only have a single fin and a head full of ideas, he concludes. a poem for the Russian girls, a dream for the ocean

thank God you ain't perfect, Paul Newman tells him. much more interesting that way.

they stand on a shanty wood balcony above the beach. The color is faded by the salt water. One way in, one way out.

ain't caught a wave in days. ain't loved a women in hours, Henry admits.

as if you are special, Paul says.

but i am, Henry weens.

they watch the sun drop into the sea; the bikini angels put their sarongs on, the last light and fugitive horizon explodes into perfection.

now thats perfection, Paul Newman says.

Sam Cooke is smiling a wise look of ridiculous understanding and wayward sensibilities from somewhere up high, where the juice is free and the girls are easy.

you still love her? Paul asks.

still love them all, Henry Castle answers quickly.

he writes to her:
miss me and all your dreams come true.
made me a fool, made me a man, and burn as i do, with all the pretension and macho hub bub. it may mean nothing to you, it may be easy, but everyday i put the Brooklyn Bridge on my back and wade out into the ocean with a dragon stick and a head full of memories, and dare The Gods to recognize me, by name and face, and drink a storm of salt water and a disco full of courage - this time around, this breathing song, makes the music fierce and the pit shine pink and blue, just as i say your name and dream of you naked and empty, in a strange hotel room, with champagne and brutal thoughts. so remember me. scream! my name and face. remember me, and let The Gods take all the words - its all for them anyway...... is this love woman? is this a full down payment?
"be married? be good?"

Sly pulls up his orange and blue stripped socks and looks in the mirror. fly, with a one way ticket to hoodlum, he thinks.

Sam Cooke sits in the corner sipping on a tall beet and carrot juice, flipping through the Bhagavad Gita and humming a James Brown track.

just in time for the disco, Sly says.

you a 365 fuck machine, Sam tells him.

all day long, all i think about is ginger tunes and girls, Sly reveals with a wide smile.

a real poet, Sam Cooke concludes. a regular bulldozer.

up all night in this beat country town, Sly says. asking for penitence and petting. everyday a shuffle closer to the casket, every night a menage with the stars.

ain't the same man i used to be, Sly continues. aint 40 acres and a smile. a damn white beach vacation close to the equator. i'm pulling nails out from the side of my empty head.

damn! she a hot little number, Cooke says, looking out of the small bedroom window onto an early evening beach. she a candy cane monsoon. and i'm a trench coat dandy, with a mean two step and a pocket full of courage.

you like me now Cooke? Sly asks sharply.

sure you do, he resolves.

Sly does a soft shoe shuffle step back onto his right foot, spins to the right, and returns to the mirror, smiling at his socks, wondering if she misses him.

don't turn the lights off, Brussel Sprout directs him. you gonna want to see this.

he stands next to the closed door and taps his foot to the sound of Santana coming from the bedroom.

now watch me bend over, now watch me fly.

in reds and blues, with the star spangled banner playing louder now, and all the second story men shuffling around the hallways, waiting for a gig.

SAND

you'll remember this, Brussel Sprout says. tell your little kids about that lady who spit fire and made you into a man.

she hovers lightly above the linoleum parkay floor and floats over to the bookshelf, where she takes down a tattered paperback book and begins to read: 'miss me and all your dreams come true.' 'made me a fool, made me a man.'

Brussel Sprout closes the book gently, then violently hurls the collection of poetry at Henry Castle.

that's for fucking her! she accuses. and thats for loving me! she spits.

she breathes fire, sets the drapes a flame, and all the servants scurry for rainwater to save the pristine library.

you may not think to look at him now, but he was famous long ago.....

all the sunshine, just waiting on the rain. juggling the solo cafe life, breathing with love and kindness - my baby has a firm handshake, and chainsaw eyes; sweet lady style has the town believing that all the stars are really shining.

but they are, Brussel Sprout says. they really are.

with one hand on the gun and the other on a wrinkled 45, she pulses into the spotlight and promises peace for all the country roads and big headed wave mavens that are praying full time down at Uluwatu.

the sun, the sun! Henry says.

my kale juice brings all the boys to the yard, she says. and now we are here......

he puts his hand behind her neck and cruises along the bottom of her hair line.

what we do for money honey, he tells her.

you are the furthest point from real cash, she says to him, and buries her chin into his chest, then exhales deeply.

perhaps this is love, he says softly.

she twists her neck to the left.

perhaps this is really fucking, she replies.

you have no idea.....

the radio plays soft:

i'm about the pursuit of happiness honey......tell me what you know about dreaming.....

Larry Levan drops a bit more disco and the kids go wild. a serious beat and a non stop heartbreak for that milky white big titty gal who is grunting her way towards the DJ booth.

its all for you, Larry mouths to her in silence. now watch this.

he cuts the last track short and abruptly drops Sex Machine. they lock eyes, and she wiggles from the top of her head to the souls of her feet. and he mouths off again: 'and if you don't know, now you know baby.'

she goes wet and shakes for Jupiter and Venus and Kali.

all you don't know, she says with her hips. all that you really wanted. thanks honey – now my stars can shine a bit brighter in this chocolate night and honey hour.

Jezzabel, she says with a smile. but all the beach boys call me J-bell.

her tight frame slides off the chair and over to the bookshelf, with a smile and a light hop.

you boys better hope i don't get all Shakespeare on ya, she kindly says. 'better to get the slings and arrows of outrageous misfortunes.....' she mis quotes with a smile.

now all you boys get in line, while i dig on these hardcover beauties, she orders.

its a disaster, Sly says.

its a fuck up, Francious adds.

just another gig, Henry Castle says. quit all your whining.

they all turn and watch Jezzabell climb the wooden ladder that runs up the towering book shelves, where she lightly fingers the spines along the top shelf.

more JD Salinger and i might cream all over this damn ladder, she says.

the boys all smile. the storm outside persists with a steady ferocity that surprises the whole peninsula.

strange strange weather, Henry observes. makes me hunger for the sunshine, and want her a little more, he whispers.

we all want her, Sly slowly adds, and stares at Jezzabell, three rings up the ladder.

nothing that cant be fixed, Francious delicately says. nothing that a rose and nuclear power plant cant repair.

you heartless romantic, Henry spits.

you lion tamer, Sly coyly says.

better speak to me with kindness today boys, Jezzabell warns. its a long paddle back to Nirvana.

Jezzabell giggles to herself and rolls the ladder further along the wall to the far end of the bookshelves, where she climbs back up to the top, and warms up next to a collection of Edgar Allen Poe paperbacks. she recalls high school sweethearts and younger ambitions.

whatever will we talk about? Francious wonders.

music, waves and girls, Sly flatly says.

the great chase, the great fires. discussing the dream that grown men sob about.

take me first Henry! Sly stands up and marches around the room, between the worn brown leather ottomans and the miscellaneous antique items.

take me first Henry! he continues. with all my beauty and fallacy and deceit. call me envious, a failed amalgamation. an expensive experiment. a perfect circle.

he scoffs at the pretension going around.

i'm just learning to be soft, Henry concludes. this love thing is so dangerously foreign to me.

Francious lights a rolled cigarette with his gold Dunhill flip top, reclines in his thick brown leather chair, and laughs fully.

another assassin, he says wisely. take the time to be broken and built again, he instructs.

the radio plays muffled from behind the kitchen doors. steady, obscure Frank Sinatra songs, barely audible.

better stoke that fire fellas, J-bell says from high up the ladder.

i just found the Marquez.......

elsewhere, Einstein digs his bare hands into a cardboard box full of foam shavings and admits his sins in blissful silence.

you better do this well, he says to himself. you better take the drop.

Henry thinks :

and you keep singing, you sexy motherfucker, as the Chilean angels dance around the vaulted room and play God to the sweet devils dressed in denim.

do you believe in love at first sight? do you feel the earth spinning faster? or have we stopped? perhaps this is the place that Ray Charles sings about. and in the more sensitive moments there is twang and heartbreak (already) for the pretty girls, who all hold hands and dance to Ruben Blades, well, with their eyes blood shot, their Botticelli faces beaming, and their heads round and perfect.

dearest lover, aging star, misunderstood philanthropist, bent over sweetheart, running pimp, the sands are all for you , the fate is sealed.....you smile and smile and smile....all she sees, all she knows. while all you wish to do is sit and weep to Pedro Navaja, while the pirates pass, and the tea strengthens.

they're probably drinking coffee, and smoking big cigars....

thick horizons, beauty and her obscene reflections, calls the beasts all home, with wild designs on freedom and service - twin generosities and genial bands of worship, keep the stars all in line, from one shoulder across to the next, torturing the water boys and their ecclesiastical howls.

not me! not me! they scream, while the horizon tastefully rises and falls, in time with the endless babbling of nature and her ravishing bulls. you continuously promise, you pray on that thirsty line and the Cajun fire, destroying memories of Big Chiefs and radical jazz heroes, between radio stations and part time jobs, skipping out on the system and her endless chores, while the pretty part time players get fat on mozzarella cheese and compare notes on hardship and pedicures.

bloated and breathing, shocked at the plastic burning fires and her wandering hips; while the music plays loud and the sensationalists agree on color schemes and dazzling locations. not your Venice Beach, not your simple dream.

and all you want to do is sing like Ruben and spit lightning with all the Bario poets.

ah, you legends, you second time around masters, your second chance at salvation and love (its all love, you tell her), and get all punchy under the harvest moon, yellow and flattering, up ahead on the highway – the stranger the better......dressed up in flowers and gold, convinced of purpose, slithering in absolution (this must be the place....) ; into a constant two step, with numbers along the forearm and promises to keep.

now beautiful, now art and sun; hanging in the mother sky, always the first time, always grabbing – you try, you try, you try – you fool, you spit and grime, so special, so upper class......the life and times of Pedro Navaja by the sea.....been there and damned, holding her blessed hand while she spins. pondering her eternal love, her infinite touch, her delicate honest earth rebuilding face, as she holds the young boy, a toddler, and sways from side to side to the sounds of South America, California, Berlin, The Bronx; and she looks into those virgin eyes and dreams of safety, peace, harmony, love – you are all i have to fix, she says with her cherry wood colored eyes; again the same, again the temptations of greatness and mercury.

you can come with me forever, she continues. and this is forever now.

somewhere between Kerobakan and Petitanget she slipped her hands around his waist and fell in love......

hard times, with the local boys and the Bukit shine; the pretty girls come and go, and Ruben steps it up a pitch – tells the Bario

Lightning Bolts and Disco Girls

story in honey and silver, with a bit of changa changa, some ass wiggling and bad ass foot tapping, make the girls dance a little bit more, from the disco room to the end of Racetracks - here again, you tell her, just to watch you spin, just to watch you smile.

always a motherfucker, always a bougie hip thrust to make sure you are listening.

its life without the pills, Ruben thinks. life on the salsa and sambal. the poor mans Tratoria, free moonshine and shiny new shorts - the neighborhood band, the Mr Heavy testaments - while Brussel Sprout hails the F train, and Henry Castle hangs with the cool kids outside the market, wondering about tricks, and other celestial contributions.

222-2222, got an answering machine that can talk to you.....

Larry Levan drops a tea bag into the cardboard cup, fills it with hot water, and summons The Gods from a wooden bench outside the Cafe Labuan. a bit more sugar please, a bit more heart.

burning, with the local fly boys and the new Bario intellectuals. hunting for acid and ginger, pushing the edge a bit further into the corners, and slipping a warm hand between her shivering thighs, again and again and again. then Bobby Darin comes over the radio, for the young local kids, so they might really get rock and roll, perhaps for the first time.

keep good company, the old man said. brings a real man to his knees, while the Canadian strippers speak about mixed drinks, and the pretty girls lose their motor bike, again and again and again.

we sit here stranded, but we are all doing our best to deny it.....

Ruben slips on the oldest 45 from the box and lets the silk get all real, for the ghosts of Frankie S and the mad wandering Bukit poets, who say it with their eyes and fuck with their hands. while Gerry Lopez holds the headstand even longer, and rails against the constitution and her wave hungry derelicts.

this life..... Henry says.

fuck this, Ruben replies.

wildest place on the planet, Henry concludes.

better with a shotgun and a set of price tags, Ruben says.

my lover ain't got no cash, Henry Castle reveals. but she holds me like a Madonna, and makes me melt for love and country. so that must be real. then we all go out into the sea, up the mountain side, out with the Grajagan tramps and the New York City harlots. takes off all the pressure and all the hate – you ain't never heard nothing like this.

the less you try the more fun it is, Ruben advices.

he slips on a dark black suit with soft shined red leather shoes and shuffles up the front steps of Madison Square Garden, with a pair of merengue dancers and court side seats to the Knicks home opener against the Boston Celtics.

he looks over innocently at the lawyers and the secretaries and the female stock brokers in gun ship grey.

never been one before, Ruben thinks to himself. must feel like Lou Reed being dragged across highway 101, with a hand full of nails and crime on the brain.

show love and you get love back, Brussel Sprout says. thats all you need to know.

and The Gods wonder where is Titus Madera? where is Woodstock? where is the love?

all love, Ruben says. just show up and let her do her thing, he continues. whistle and shout, from the Bukit to the Boogie Down. the endearing milkshake shaka shaka; the interesting sexy; let the Bukit angels get their penicillin shots and saintly seasonal prizes.

hati hati young man; the beach knows your name, Ruben tells him. just another water junky in the mix....fabulous as Pedro Navaja, dope as the rain.

Henry settles into a blood red banquet at the back of an affluently lit room and orders a carrot juice from a short Latina waitress who looks tired and eternally bored.

same dull crowd, he thinks to himself. same stuffed shirts.

Lightning Bolts and Disco Girls

same midnight mockery and bogus aspirations.

he is steadily sinking into the abyss when the Latina sweetheart brings a fresh carrot juice and a small white porcelain bowl filled with edamame.

he enjoys the constant buzz of city in the room. the new age billionaire hippies, the newsroom celebrities, the hedge fund hipsters, the flailing Russian model girls waiting for the beauty to stop.

we are all here, Henry thinks to himself.

he enjoys these short trips to Babylon.

he waits for two hours, drinking juice alone in the back, watching the human carnival flip and rhyme. imagining various gangster scenarios while A Love Supreme plays on repeat, yet no one seems to mind.

outside the cold air sets in, finally, with November limping along, frugal down the avenues and side streets; the melancholy parks and across the confident bridge systems. kiss and run, pash and dash – the girls roll up in furs and cloth: Burberry bankrupt patterns and rosy cheeks that causes the vamp red lipstick to spread and wander.

those perfect celestial faces and Roman expectations, following the money, always a good time, Henry thinks.

always another dope party, while Miki flicks the needle and Jasper settles in with the paint brush. a long evening of agony and homage. ya cold baby? you need anything?

the prize fighters take a table up front, blocks out the whole brass section, but no one says a word.

Max Roach strolls out looking ambivalent and masterful. ain't nothing i ain't done before, his body language says straight. ain't no where i ain't been.

just in time for the 1AM set, while the hop heads settle in and the margaritas go around the VIP section.

he starts with a solo. an alone piece, a testament. we be here after the boats, on the other side of the river, thin and hungry, with all this sick around me, and all these shackles on my wrists. the boat just keeps on , with that rise and fall, maligned and wanted, stripped of dignity and virtue, with all the other dark slabs of meat and spectacular acts of heartbreak and destiny; imagine someplace closer to the beach, where up on the hill its all clear, just sky and the floating horizon, where the buttercups dance and the winds hum a melody clear for the ears of children and dreamers.

imagine the fresh air again, instead of this stale dead air, this slave greatness, this stoic prospect. he plays slow and melancholy. the cries continue, the stress is heroic; the faithless moans and shivering hours simply pass, while the clouds of hate and anguish blanket the hilltops, and rain dragon's fire on all the walking flowers.

this is love, Max plays. this is survival.

bash bash bash, Monty Monty yuk; dragging me down, but i still get a gig: the late spot on Saturday nights, the cat who brings all the philanthropists around after midnight. no worries sweetheart, he plays. listen to this: tik tik tik tik tik tik, bsh, bah bsh, kapah kapah kapah......

here i be master, in all my flames, all my dress.

Max picks up the pace. with a proper London tailored suit and a cheap pair of New York City shoes. push push, bash bash – we may be ripped and sore, but this snare drum speaks of the Euphrates and her hungry joy; waltzing across a long twisting memory, with sleeping children and promises of love.

tap tap tap; Max Roach nods towards the thin two man horn section, and they wake up fast and get ready for the big come on.

hear me again sweetness, Max whispers. we are all here, just having a good time, just breathing fire.

all fedora hats and absolute 4th street jive....jiggle jiggle, sweet sweet; check this gold, the easy drop, the history of slaves and ghosts – now i'm a motherfucker, the black prince, the last nigger in a tweed jacket and a suede chocker collar. now i'm *the* man, the tax man, the monument and the moon. come back home

Lightning Bolts and Disco Girls

sunshine, only so much sorrow a young streetwalker can take.

Max does his thing, again, plowing through time, from the observation deck of the Empire State Building, looking out past the Hudson River, over the pulsing slab of Manhattan, the waste lands of Jersey, missing the Twin Towers and all her majesty. for that American girl.....

what are you *doing*? Brussel Sprout asks, watching wanton lovers pass, with other brutish men, and dying again.

hati hati and jazz, a bit faster, into it, jab jab, body blow body blow; then back up and jive; left then right, watch the sweet feet shuffle; mama mama, dash dash, lost and gone; smile a bit, more and wonder – you gotta die sometimes – a fine day to be born again.

just be cool bro, The Gods whisper. Tidak apa

be cool motherfucker! Miles demands. you here always.

Henry Castle paddled out alone, slightly exhausted and apprehensive.

your thrill, he thinks. your windy tomb. your seven day madness.

the winds turned early, as they do this time of year. he watched the waves from the beach for a short time before deciding to take the longer paddle to the south side, where the waves looked more chaotic, but fewer people.

arrested by the sun and sand, burning; the heavens call and the pretty dark clouds linger, longer and longer.

she said, i had no idea you were so new agey.

new agey......

Henry told her about his father and the swamis and the letters and the Ashram in India that burnt to the ground and has never been rebuilt because the ground is still too hot to stand on.

and she smiled.

he told her about the city seminars and long afternoons at the book shops, mediation under the Birch trees; the balance between sharp rugged business and wild Zen philosophies;

Indian traditions and ornate ceremonies that keep the sky blue; giant crystals everywhere that keep the urban energy clean. the money and the contracts, that litter the tables and shackle the destiny.

the vibrations, he tells her. roll with the vibrations. take a chance, fall in love more; take the drop when you don't want to; walk around bare foot, stay out of the system, listen to the Grateful Dead the whole ride up, he tells her. he reminds *himself.*

Henry packs up the single fin long board and a smaller fat board into a thick green surf board bag with a small tear in the tail. he adds two large fins, one smaller fin, a set of quad fins, leashes, screw driver, wax, zinc, leash ties, booties, a rubber vest, The Yoga Sutras, a bag of cashews, two black t shirts, two flower patterned Hawaiian shorts, a long sleeve button down flannel shirt, and a light jacket for the nights.

on the drive north Henry sings Friend Of The Devil softly, and weaves through the night traffic, with all his baggage hanging off the sides, and a few bucks in his pocket.

super casual, a bit of push, just ride it out, he tells himself. a kiss and a turn; more smiles, more laughter.

you are so serious, The Gods tells him.

you are so peaceful, he replies.

where is the love? he asks. what has happened to the love?

the beach shines, then thick jungle, then patches of Western development.

better to be a wonderful water bum then a concrete town masquerader, Henry thinks to himself.

the stage is set: the young bikini girls and their sacred commitment to blind excitement – get it down, let it slide out. Henry watches the pretty girls come and go, while the healers walk in like queens in neoprean and casually lead the salt boys into the bedrooms.

"like a tree planted by the side of the river i shall not be moved."

the preacher gets into it. dips down, slowly rises back up, and explodes - the whole theater screaming. the rapture, the swine and heat and gore. the man in a black suit with a dark olive green tie and newly shined crocodile shoes roars, and all the white men sit and listen; newly destroyed, recently found.

this is what we do, the preacher says to himself, in the late evening, alone in his tent, counting his cash. this is really happening.

AUM AUM, hati hati; dig these threads, check this walk.

the healer walks out with a pocket full of hundreds and all the vibrations turn green again. my roadside beauty, my constant darling, he says to himself. cut and spicy - another tough fucking Jordy - he sinks in and goes special; the long work week and disco saturday night special.

ram ram sita ram.

again the whack jobs hit the road.

when they arrive its all waves and sex; red ants, peace and Zed Zeppelin. 'whatever you think you are you really are,' The Gods repeat.

the ghost of Allan Watts, a chubby Ginsberg, and a bleeding Moses stroll down the stairs and make peace with the wild girls, the absent fathers, the shop boys and the cool longboard trixies who profess midnight love and other disasters.

from the bookcase to the DJ booth, back in the Treme its all bounce and Bintangs, while up on the hill its mellow 7 o clock cool, as Gerry gets suited up and the reiki nymphs order another chocolate martini from the tranis down on 11th avenue.

you look like a star, Jezzabell tells a newly arrived random, walking up the reef with a wet long board and head full of defeat.

you'll do for a night of disco and slide guitar, she tells him

are you overwhelmed yet? Brussel Sprout carelessly asks Henry. are you angry yet?

thankful, Henry says.

Brussel Sprout lays in bed reading The Wall Street Journal and listening to Ruben Blades on the FM radio.

  luck and money, Henry thinks. here we go.

  mighty assassin attributes and the time to make it all better. act like you know The King; smile at the yuppies, eating all the peanut butter.

  how mellow can you get? Brussel Sprout wonders. how cool are you?

  how free is it all – really? Henry wonders.

  little float, beauty and the boogie, wrapped up in another dream, with a fade, a big bamboo stick, alone for the moment, a hippy tune and a bag of ginger.

  sama sama, The Gods sing in unison. a fine performance.

  easy palm tree, gentle sun, mellow wind, cool day; in your peaceful hands, above the shore, floating through time. your merry ways, your giant speach – in that deep silence, in that golden hue, winging it; again easy, as you do....with the hippy swingers and the colorful surfboards; the generous intrigue and the marvelous soul (all soul, still.....); where the lovely ladies come to chat and the pirates come to vacation.

  warm, perfect, beautiful – as the alchemy roots in, and the barber shop quintets chants Om Namah Shivaya. a clear blue sky, nothing but that empty charm, works every time.

  the poets finally arrive and dig the scene. where the revolutionaries lay down their books and swords and feel the plain savage sunshine soothe the weary lines on their weathered faces.

  so radical, so lovely – the decisions we make, the roads we choose.

  its not about you, its about us, Einstein repeats wisely.

  meet me in new New Orleans, Max casually tells Henry.

  they stand around the back of the club, with the tin garbage cans and the blinking red lights. where the music plays all day and night, and the waves are always breaking. gum ball mama, milky heartbreak, another stop on the tour, another potential home.

where is the party at? Max asks Henry. dressed in red, ready to consume.

the masters bring clarity, as the salts seep in, and the mamas catch a few waves on the inside.

groovy at sunrise, sitting peaceful out the back, dreaming of Lopez and those long Java days; a little late to the show, but still here.

the peace is astounding, Henry thinks. calm. without doing much. you find another slice of land to call home, next to the foreign cowboys with the big smiles and the out of state plates. you are bold, delicious, insane, with a bit more foam (you learn) as the modern day flappers trot down the beach and cue up closer to the peak every time.

a few visions, a few breaths. in the distance the sounds of hammers burying nails in the Redwood trees. out to the horizon the same celestial sunrise, the warm conclusion, the wet acrobatics, the numb exchanges and obese mornings. and now we are free, and now we are beautiful.

the neighbors are all having sex, and the battered besties are bathing with their fellow barbarians down by the beach. Bobby Dylan plays mellow and slow from inside – all radical, all outside the system, on the endless tour, with the alchemists and the nomadic necrophiliac groupies.

we will be here forever, thats what all the t shirts say.

take a bit of sunshine, add ginger and rose, with rock and roll along the rim, slightly pampered and all push – the destitute angels of time and water, who have the whole day to wait and ponder.

Kerouak's lonely fire tower moved beachside.

when the paparazzi arrives, have them use the side door, leave cash on the bedside table; hear the country tunes, and watch the longboard gospel kids kick it to the butterflies between sessions.

hati hati, you tell them. such a fun way to spend the years.

though somewhere Woodstock is calling. the great open space, the wild mountain rhymes; the temple and the broken innocence. she calls it beautiful lady poetry, absolute water, divine flower, lovely smile, hot and restless.

Henry surrenders, as Krishna's voice becomes clearer, and the space to hear it opens and invites you in.

Henry Castle listens to the water run in the shower. he pictures her milky bare body, her bright chestnut eyes and heartbreak hands, jumping between lovers and social obligations, with credit cards maxed out and the mounties searching the high planes for that rolling darling face.

here again, he thinks. blessed and peaceful, with no guitar to play and the ink running out. sweet solace in the sunshine, elegant on the hill tops. wonder how she looks dressed up? he thinks. wonder what all the gentleman debutants would say?

if you promise me freedom then i will promise you happiness. thats all she ever says.

made me a fool, easing into the deep end. the fading cafe scenes, the withering vegetable greens, puts all the fly girls on notice.

and it begs the question: what are you doing? what difference do you make? as the communities rise and fall, we all keep running.

always a fan of the great revolutionaries: Malcolm, Martin, Mahatma – and we sit here now, basking, drowning, looking at our photos, our water, and the tears continue to fall, and the boys crush them stones under the glaring midday heat.

the fortunate bastards, the tender motherfuckers, the easy rider longboard expeditions; to return groovy and awake, in love, believing. to stand for something important, to believe in something big. explore and break away, strongly, where there are no signs – heroes and cowboys......a sly extension of those weary urban ways, with all the honey beauty dripping across those empty green steeped rice fields, while the soldiers keep moving along, endless, insane, weary, wet, simply passing, all left over, all bitching, all piled up and for sale.

while the high end artists deftly pretend, one hand on the heart and the other on the trigger. frightfully fit and without direction – taken, abused by water, reading the signs.

we are what we pretend to be, Alan says again. now throw out the trash and bend over a bit deeper.

with heartless pangs of love, and stretching gaits of beauty, Henry Castle relents into the burning scene, while the vacation girls sit under the bright lights and eat Italian food.

satu lagi, Sly orders.

Max effortlessly swings into a slow ballad version of Salt Peanuts, that makes the Swedish beauty queens reach for their wallets.

Ganesh wakes up early, just after first light. she dresses in the middle of the single room she shares with Brussel Sprout. a simple red bathing suit, and a tired face. committed.

keeps you out of trouble, she thinks.

the silence wraps them tightly. we go here then there, around and around, brilliant, spectacular, misfits – the outside looks chilly yet promising. no doubts, no second thoughts.

she slides down the beach unassuming, measuring her silence in decades, and when she enters the water it starts to rain, and it never stops.

the dreamers all come out to look, from a high, steep landing atop the low limestone cliffs. they hum in admiration, shrouded in excellence; one giant family, one true faith. better not want anything else, they sing in unison. a bit of love, a bit of compassion.

with a smile, simple, looking at the sun, back out the same way you came in – all darkness and wonders. perched up high, doing it, grateful in the warm morning light. the lines of humanity, the growling, towards something, that looks special, light and free.

SAND

the water crashes against the beach, without concern, over and over again. while the Buddhists chant OM TAT SAT, and the disco balls rev up for another shot at the tittle.

marked for fabulous, again a sign and a breath, before and after the love and loss and wild debacles. left furious and beautiful. you've survived, the stars all say, in their own bright tongues. they wipe your forehead clean, relieved, and happily broke.

someone has to mind the store; someone has to pay the bills. locally tuned, forever happy, easily amused, dynamite in the sack. glowing Buddha saint, with candles, ginger and rhyme. awake, from the hometown to the rice fields. blessed and relieved, smile at the strangers, we are all in love, we are all happily dying, François admits.

just passing through, Henry says to the lynch mob. don't mind me, the hook and snare. just looking for an outlet, just hoping for a plug. this wild attachment, this peaceful penitentiary. all gorgeous in the jungle, all feisty and unbelievable. give it all back and hope that none of those pretty girls catch you sniffing around the dump.

the music plays low in the other room, as it should. The White Stripes, from a live concert album, from the previous decade. much distortion and reverb, screeching songs and a grueling organ sound. the drums pound with disdain, further up and up the jittery coast, through a chorus about true love, about pain; and Jack is pulling his hair out, and the crowd erupts, and the guitar bites, with electricity and designer rebellion. all the way to an abrupt stop, as the waves crest and fall into a sudden silence.

AUM! he cries loudly. and the crowd goes wild.....

Larry Levan sits in the departures lounge at Chaing Mi airport counting the number of Asian women in the room.

soon its warm, then cold, then warm again, he thinks to himself. best time ever.

he sips from his porcelin cup filled with beetroot juice and yawns mightily.

what day is it? he wonders. how did i get here?

there is an announcement over the loudspeaker, and the two Asian women sitting across from him abruptly stand up and wheel their matching suitcases towards the exit door, without a word.

all the beautiful saints, try not to rush in and out; still the freedom in the trees and in the wind. still the revelation of flowers and sunshine; still the soft happy sounds of clouds and air. still the rejuvenating touch of dirt and sand.

brought all the fortunes of history, time, and the full blade of expectation, Ganesh thinks.

what a mischievous heartbreak; a melancholy sorrow, yet an exuberant time. at least that is what all the lotus flowers tell me.

a dash of power, trouble, illumination; time spent under a rock, time spent burned in the sand.....release the daily screams and covetous moans – the blue sky luxuries, the cool air and wailing shadows. The Gods love you, but shut the fuck up.

freedom – again the store, again the iron. a glass of broccoli, a bit of tofu, at the edge of euphoria, and all the pretty dollar bills just burn on the empty blue horizon.

air on the side of wild, Ganesh instructs wistfully. its is all Plan A.

never boring, she demands.

vegetarian rogues, scholars, beauties – never fear, all in, all here. Mr Heavy cracks a smile.

for what reason? Sly genuinely asks.

for the tradition, and the nature, Brussel Sprout resolutely responds.

its a sunshine day again, and the boulevards and the beaches fill up lovely, with wandering faces and sex crazed bandits. water water, sand sand – bend the back, alleviate the fear – its all good Uncle Sam, no worries Little Homeslice.

honest and moaning, Henry sits and smiles. encouraging,

outrageous, free of envy; in paschimottanasana, and all the dirty emotions shoot through his legs.

a simple mack truck, a melancholy baseball game to pass the years. alive and kicking, the madness is tonic, the surf reports keep filing in......hati hati Mr CEO, mellow and peacefully outrageous – the greens fill the body and demand clean uplifting satisfaction, as the days roll by and the palm trees sway over Oberoi.

the new punk museum, the surfer grave yards; the naked virgins aside the cliffs of Uluwatu. play the tune slow and pretty.........

I am old enough to remember the jazz section at Tower Records, Henry tells a table full of strangers down by the beach. the coolest place in the universe.

all enthusiastic on cool, all up on curiosity – clean oceans and loving line ups; peaceful streets and blessed mountain tops. warm and tender, the toughest motherfuckers have their equipment together, while the boys run around and watch the saints dance all Sunday night.

calmly counting mala beads and watching the beautiful girls drink coconut water directly out of the shell, Henry sits and wonders, about the wild old lovers and make out kings.

better bring the cast and the credit cards, he thinks. this one has lots of style.

never dull, plowing through the pretension and mediocrity – James Dean i heart you; Johnny Depp i apologize.

but fuck it, nobody really knows. but everybody cares.

satvic and sexy, running around all day trying to fuck older American women. such great breasts, Henry thinks to himself. alone and silent.

i would devour you, he tells her, naked, an open palm on her bare hip. this is what we love, he tells her. this is who we are.

where did all the money go? Henry wonders. is this what we do with our time? he thinks.

calm, the lights go on and off, for the celebrity virgins and lonely school girls. for the rich little women who jump and

Lightning Bolts and Disco Girls

jump; for the dream......the lovely undying wet dream.

take me now! Cat Women screams at a half naked mysterious Brazilian boy.

the penetration penthouse, Sprout speaks into her smart phone. come right in.

take a breath, let it all roll by...... The Gods are amused.

better get a bigger bank account for that piece of ass, Sly says. while Leopold smiles in agreement, and Henry nods understandingly.

those poor little rich girls love the diamonds and the dirt, Sly preaches. you keep it real, stand by your beliefs, and some lowly darling will sweep in and rescue you right back, Sly professes to Henry.

you keep fucking around like this and you gonna die, Leopold tells the boys.

ain't like it hurts, Henry tells the wet choir boys. aint like walking around wanting it all the time.

the vortex is a shell game. the food is cheep, ethical; full time fuck machines – the addicts take to the field, the freedom is napalm. my loose fearless darling, my chocolate maker in the sand. rock and roll plays soft, the sox get pulled way up. your own pitching style, your own late night talk show, for the girls to see.....

two days locked in a hotel room in a random city, Henry tells her. i like the rich girls, he says. every position you've wanted to try. no begging, no mercy – constant and cumming, always in and out.

the mind blows soft through the open windows and the sun has decided to show all day. all in and dangerous, all the reputations ruined, thankfully.

a full time motherfucker, a lightning bold (again), in the steeped history of salt water sliding and dance floor cowboys.

take her tonight, Henry, Sly tells him. she really needs it. even better if you don't kiss her.

SAND

the music plays soft, hometown acts and legendary temperaments. The Boss slides by, the hip girls all roll in. my hometown, my easy way and warm urban style, Henry thinks. no way out, no problems. all night, up for skinny dipping; just admit how much fun it is.

he is naughty Ganesh says, from a steady perch on top of a bear skin rug in Las Vegas.

he still has no idea, Cat women says.

longboards and love machines, deceivingly simple.

precious open air and salty maturation; the sound repeated of ocean and such; a holy pinnacle at the beach - so open and free, such blessed silence. there are no words for this - the blissful suicide, the cool walk and constant surprise - love and go, the upper echelons of mellow - the endless ways to be free.

exposure, warm, the air is smiling, the wind is the only real free component in town. can't buy anymore ocean, can't claim anymore glory. the detox and the beauty - the longer we go, the greater we are. sad perfection, exhumed expectations - the service is all anyone remembers - straight talking and tattooed in all the right places.

thoughtful as a razor blade, hard as a brick. always love love love, always sex sex sex - behind those chestnut eye, in bed with another man, handy around the house; just someone to care about you, just some more pleasure please.

strength, measured in smiles, paid by the hour; a few books for the beach girls, a random act of sensitivity for the dragon.

here for the holidays, Brussel Sprout tells a new crowd. home with the pirates, surprised by melancholy and tangerines, raging at the corner boys who tried to make a difference, with visions of Gill Scott Heron and the yuppie princes who portend to be hard..... measured in steps towards the nose, silent in the corner, echoing the sentiments of mother nature and Miles Davis.

don't look, you bad motherfucker, Sly suggests. might get blinded by all that temptation.

the beach holiday that destroyed you, the best little patch of shade; the great seaside hustle, the banging razor blade who wont let you go.

hati hati – its all a big game........

sink, those gangster eyes and window shopping savants – you can have the beauty or the orgy, but can't have both, The Gods warn.

restless in the late morning sun, blasphemous in the dark; trim down the glossy rhetoric for the sunset sessions, up and down the New York State Thruway, for the love and other lacerations.

her story is the same as yours, just shorter, Henry thinks. crack an egg, drop the 45's. all geeky, far out and clean – the wedding bells will have to wait, its Christmas in the jungle. hati hati, you may meet someone nice......

Brussel Sprout offers to pick up the tab, but Leopold insists its his round. nobody argues, nobody cares anymore.

and what if i just get up and go, Brussel Sprout announces suddenly, leaping to her feet, sweating, her voice cracking.

and what if i just implode, she continues. who is going to love you all then, huh? she asks. you filthy motherfuckers.

Leopold adds up the bill and throws down whatever is left in his pockets. he takes a last pull of club soda from a large wine glass, leans across the table, and kisses Magdelena square on the mouth.

you all can have her, Leopold announces. i'm in love with the eternal......

the table erupts in cheers, except for Brussel Sprout, who throws an empty wine glass at the wall and yells "BOO! BOO!"

who told you to sell out, Sprout yells above the cheers. who told you to fall in love, again!

Larry Levan pleads the fifth, and abruptly plays Part Time Lover, with the treble dropped out.

free blow jobs for all the local boys! Catwomen tells the balcony bums. and everyone stands up.

SAND

The Gods just watch.

loose with the adjectives, easy on the eyes, the professional girls arrive by the dozen, and spend Christmas in the jungle. high on spirit, long legs and wealthy.

the green is all you've got, Henry thinks, but then corrects himself.

love and more love, The Ocean says. showing up as a fan, leaving as a hero. for all its worth, empty pockets and all; top of the world, important in all the tight places. illuminated and naughty, fresh with with the hands, seriously to the left, from Greenwhich Avenue to Patagonia; from Wall Street to Beat Street; from Union Square to Labuan Sait; the holiday pills have all worn off, and the Buddhas are seated up at the bar, bobbing their heads to Larry's latest track.

yeah you turn me........

the dance floor erupts, the beach explodes, the pueblo is white hot.

mucho mucho, Henry wonders. maybe Brussel Sprout found herself someone nice.

in the haze of another warm afternoon, Einstein sits at the round metal table, alone in the room, rolling a cigarette and drinking cheap instant coffee.

its all come to this, he sourly thinks.

The Ocean raises her head and shoots him a wink. Einstein manages a thin smile.

ok, he says. you got me. now lets get to work.

Lightning Bolts and Disco Girls

NORTH OF PARADISE

*

Her clean blue eyes, and the sound of babies crying; the sun slowly descends - where on earth am I? Literally, could not place it on a map; all the way north for a quiet time alone - this is where the emergency exit is, this is where the oxygen is, this is me pretty - hug, and watch me walk. Jalam jalam....that is all i know.

All rivers through Rome - how many more minutes on my phone? Double check, the cleaning lady looks dodgy. Henry watches her closely, hungry; it is known for being loose around here.

"Walked out the front door this morning and was fully greeted by two flaming gay dudes and a super hot hooker chick, and they were all like 'hey, hey boy, what are you doing?' She was smoking hot," Mr Heavy says.

The restaurant smells like pig and clorox. The local gangsters, in colorful shirts, sit at a long corner table and divvy up the souls. The buffet is cleared away, the music is fast and instrumental, with Mark Whalberg on the flat screen television next to the exposed brick oven pizza kitchen.

Remnants of empires and hand me down fashion; speaking with God, smoking cigarettes and drinking sugar. Better to have some straight pussy then fuck around with these hookers all the time, the voice says. Through the ether, the pirate hot line, persistent in water and penetration – the pirate diaries, the Jim Carrol crucifixion. Come back to me Paris, all fashion and cleavage; come back to me New York City, all money and walk. Come back to me Bali, all Gods and garbage.

The pressures of a rotating earth, singing the verses, lost in the fine creases of ejaculation – here we go, a puddle jumper to the island, a cruise control expose – goodbye grains of sand, goodbye Hollywood..... casting 101, the dream in black and white, the film grainy, the music that made the lifestyle: white boy twang and ghetto rebellion, smart and fit.

"They put up these flags and get a couple of drinks and some music and some girls and say lets have a competition, lets have a party......" Where do we go from here? Mr Heavy wonders. Straight into that French girl, straight into that quiet tiny villa by the sea, he surmises.

Away great ocean, away great melody! Henry hears the voices, fearful, seducing him.

Pondering the island's deteriorating future, the capitalist destiny on dry land, where all the criminals hang. No, but really, its a motherfucker......

She walks around the waiting room in tight high rise jean shorts, straight for the free food. Dark skin, with a tattoo on her upper thigh, dirty and glorious. On her way to an island somewhere, no one knows she has gone, no one knows she is alone. Escapism, that is where the beauty happens.

Again the smell: fried cheese, egg and fish.

Henry waits, on the worn green couches and low slung stylish brown arm rest fuck it chairs. He waits, behind the glass, a few steps from the tarmac, easy on the eyes. Out there where the dream is, out there where the chips are cashed. Quiet, as the sky dissolves behind a polluted hangar, and the sharks choke on retail chains and hastily placed billboards. An honest moment alone, mellow, all to get there, all to find out...... Where did she go?

Henry wonders.

He spots her, back in the corner, alone, eating in sweat solitude, weary of the pirates and the soldiers; then a quick strut around the food counter – what could you possibly say to entice a tiger? he wonders. 'Treat me badly, so i remember you later on.'

Gone again, patient in the afternoon heat; not the Panamanian border crossing, not the putt putt tisk tisk of Northern Arizona. Pressed and testing – balance the memories, respect the Gods.

Good people, high level angels, elevated ambitions, simple play things. Low tech toys and long term munchies, without the risk. Calling home again, the 70's style VIP airport lounge glows emerald green.

Look around: the white dude in the New York Knicks t-shirt. Believe.

Henry pauses. Its all gonna be great.

They are dancing wildly outside the box, enjoying hot tea in another world, wild. Wild for the sun and sand. Where did that Brazilian girl go? She walked towards the yellow smoking room with a camera tripod and a hard case on wheels. Damn. Just this simple breathing will be fine, Henry concludes. Thank you very much.

Home town teams – are you a fan? Henry wonders. Are you a doctor? Is it a mistake? Do you have any idea?

Standing around the garden at 730pm, bottom of the club elevator, positioned away from the rising crowd, the formal push, the animal city; the suits, the rap stars and the rich kids; waiting for a date, a girl, a speck of blood, an ounce of dirt.

Here we go, into the heart, the multi mogul slot machine, the worlds most famous arena; the smell of popcorn and hard wood floors – gloss and money; the shine, clean and brilliant, the orange heart, the blue blood, the black style – elevated, hard and beautiful. He solemnly remembers it all, from a dirty low slung plastic chair, far away.

Mr Heavy and the white heavies talk waves and islands: the side industry (the circus) comes rolling through. They conclude: the saviors, the death star, the light grind and makable sections. The older dudes with cash swap itineraries: exotic, exclusive, quiet; the places you want to visit, the names you like to hear.

please baby baby, please baby baby, please......

All rock star and branded bling, all plans and future ambitions. Mr Heavy makes moves from the executive airport lounge. A blackberry and another dream: bigger and blacker, with every blessed day that passes, bowing to the abundant universe, stylish, in red and black.

That is strange, Henry notices. The beautiful Brazilian girl traveling alone, in a place like this, to a place like that. Trade secrets and lust abound; clean white t-shirts and well fit baseball caps. The evolution of feral, the real progression. Synchronized expat living: white skin, a bit of money, a sexy local girl who smiles a lot.

The reason to be in Jakarta, Mr Heavy explains. The reason we go anywhere...

Globe trotting, with an extensive network of madmen, ready to jump head first into the void. Marvelous, unemployed saints and cruising heavenly groupies. Drinking straight gasoline, putting it into drive, dancing on the edge, made for speed, and style.

The Brazilian paces the waiting lounge, cut free and floating, awesome under the lights.

En route to the island, they hit the ocean. Goodbye coastline, a few thousand feet up, when Led Zeppelin comes on. No diving, no pressure – positive vibrations, 4-6ft and clean. Wave your hand at Ahab – he is winking at you.

A little bit of an evening party, a whisper and a kiss – good evening water, electric, the plans and mega hobbies – center stage young man, mellow and clean. The fresh air, the wonder. Listen to the ocean and feel the breeze, the bass line, the miracle. The boys stare off into space, emphatic in salt, mesmerized by the horizon, the hunt, the style (again, the style....), with an interesting opinion, with a hungry crew of veterans frothing.

Gorgeous water queen and groovy, she brings the house down. A little bit more push, and at night the pirates find solace in the silence and the flame. Here again.

Mr Heavy takes a blade from off the midnight flyer and stares the forecast down a bit, because no one knows what is going to happen. Its a miracle, its Hamlet down at the beach. Peaceful, easy, and insane – purged, away from her, and her, and her........

Negotiations over candle light, promises at gun point. Summits by the beach, heroes for the poor. They dream.

Its bigger then initially forecasted, Mr Heavy announces.

It rounds the universe and sleeps on the sand. Chases the shore line, from pole to pole. Puts a weary head between lazy tan thighs and goes to work. The height of the game, for the simple love of fresh air and freedom.

It is as free as anything these days, Henry concludes.

That is what we are supplying, Mr Heavy says. Safe freedom and clean sheets

Ready for that close up, Henry thinks. Ready for that chainsaw.

They spoke about freedom, they spoke about The Crusades.

Almighty, please protect these wonderful people; please allow the karma credit to go through. The Saphos go looking for waves, all along the South West coast of the island, from one beach to the next, considering swell direction and wind and size. They take close out beach poundings, to make all the sin disappear. So excellent, so easy. Not a bother, not a complaint.

Clean living, The Captain says.

Yes, simple simple, they conclude. Even when its steep and closing.

Get up and make a home, the voices they conspire. Get up and promise the world – the envy of all the boys, the pro forma deal to make it legitimate. Who else do we need validation from? Tell me it is good, whisper you love me.

Easy on the eyes, mellow on the distractions. A little wood bungalow by the beach, hoping that prayers for the late Michael Peterson are heard. Continually convinced its all perfect, staring at the 7.6 candy board with love and awe and excitement. Stretching the all forgiving arms around the 80's summer time blues, waiting to paddle out. Hati hati baby. Love it when she says it, slow and affectionately. Hati hati baby, in all your chest bulging splendor, with the hard stuff and cheap French cologne permeating in the easy late afternoon sunshine.

Henry bows his head as he enters the water. Prayers for François and Einstein, before the ocean takes her cut – in the jungle baby, in the jungle. The boys walk around barefoot and branded, convinced of their commitment to water and wave. A head nod, a bit of cool, stretched out and pretty against the timeless horizon. Personable and equipped for happiness.

Here we go, Henry whispers.

Again, here we are, in the shade and shadows, breathing a bit of life into that lost and rugged generation of saints and spinsters, no look cowboy store addicts, with nothing but money and time. A bit of life in the voice, kindly requesting silver and smiles, long kisses and fresh cooked vegetables over brown rice (we are vegetarians!). With a new song and an old pair of socks to make you shiver from far away.

Mental, divine, charging....fancy and free (trying, maybe yes); hippie all up and down this damn God island. All up in orange, all fabulous in blue.

The holistic approach: beans and toast, grilled tomato and juice. A bride returned from the jungle, a little organic groovy, a little water paradise. Yes, talking straight at you; all the lovely glow and moon, the sunshine rising in the clear pale blue sky. Just a bunch of kids relishing in water and style – trying hard, and the wave still broke out the back.

Mr Heavy grabs his shortboard and marches out to the sea; the first day of Ramadan, the hip hop beats and human silence still fresh in his soul. Offshore winds and glass; six people out on the peak, patient and skilled, potential energy and kinetic dreams. Put the dream on repeat, say the mantra: 'peace and love', a lot. We came here to sing, we came here to relax.

Everybody just relax! The Captain yells, and all the local boys turn sheepish, and admit their sins.

Just a little ranch on the beach, just a cool place to hang...... Get inside, the bastions of inner peace and constant song – mellow with the tides, easy at the edge of the world. Again silence, again grass. Pushing legitimacy up a steep hill – undecided, mental, strong; a beast, a baby.

All the local kids flood into the road after early morning prayer. First light, profound and committed. In packs: the young boys tiny and ragged, full of mischief and impoverished curiosity. The girls covered in colorful burkhas, they walk slow and gossip, weaving close to the shoulder of the road, charmed and pure. The light hits the ocean and grows (a beginning, again). Here comes the machine, here is the giant.

Let the juice settle in, Henry decides. Let the molecules take hold. A flood of energy. All successfully one, when the evening session arrives.

Around the coast and up the beach The Saphos have been hunting and battling; every ripple, every thought. When they settle back into the camp, finally calm and still, the forecast promises a good time.

Hanging local and pumping, that's what Mr Heavy predicts.

The kid plays the guitar outside the kitchen. A straight four bar blues on a faded acoustic body with rusty strings. The Saphos get ready. The boat comes and goes. There are still dudes out on the peak.

Hati hati, Henry tells The Saphos.

Cool. The only english word Mr Heavy teaches the local kids.

The winds blow lightly. Biggie Smalls comes on the radio, then Ice Cube.

As long as the winds stay offshore, as long as the cut closes up clean – its a heavy mansion made of wood boards and dirt – its another mission; the simple path: the kid went down South and took a couple on the head – all in a mornings work – keep it light. The heavy heavy, the wind – and off again to the airport, for the critical point in the plan – the mucho mucho, the languishing local burka girls with the wise smiles and the crooked teeth.

Good morning little wild blue world; good morning photographer. Good morning tea, as the tide starts to rise, and the ocean continues to hum, and the sleepy faces wake and wander through, misty and committed.

The day begins a new; a dream, a visit. The blue chatter and white water, so crude and violent; a pretty lady on West 4th Street, a mobile lover and no Wifi service.

Keep it down! Mr Heavy bellows.

The gas lamps, the patriarch – another pseudo charm – awake young prince, first time outside the castle, wandering the side roads and sewer streets, again appalled by the mess and the lingering lust, again enthralled by the rock and water and rags; again a mysterious turn to empty, basking in the light dance and brilliant song.

Outside the castle walls with the blood and the cursing and the after birth. Outside the castle with the queers and the fanatics and the car bombs. Outside the castle with the DJ's and the guides and the water whores. Outside the castle with a stack of dirty cash and a pocket full of lollipops. Again outside the castle with fresh fruit, clean waves, blades of wild grass, and infinite kisses, liberated and honest; a proper send off, a bit of time to learn the ropes.

Humble, in a quiet town, easy by the beach, planting more trees and bursting with love – our hero steps forward and watches the horizon, with keen interest and gentle time (tugging, away with a breath and a grin); up Leviathan! up Cadillac Ranch!

Minimum wage and pimping, chasing the beast and wondering, for a moment, for a song.

I hear a train a coming, its rolling round the bend, and i ain't heard the sunshine since, i don't know when.......

Compliments to the chef, Henry tells The Captain. Cold breakfast and fast waves - punk rock and lead - holy holy, the price of glory, the arrow and the branch.

Henry envisions muscle car amphetamines, open minds and dirty thoughts (oh, France, oh modesty, oh naked fingered beauty queen aging and smug - over it, and willing to screw for food); oh lover, oh enemy; so punching the clock, so scantily clad and dreaming of love and wine and easy pulls and shining jewels.

The heroes arise, everyone is suffering - fussed with fat thighs and a model's scandalous pose - saunter in, check the waves, make some thin plans, hear the music, pleasure the beast.

In a dream:

Sleepy and somber, the boys are praying for water and enlightenment. They are packing for the trip to Northern India. Gave away the quiver, relinquished the wet life. Gave up the girls, the dancing, the swells, to view the storied waterfalls of pure prana, and the levitating wise men in robes, smiling and silent. For the bursts of light and holy chants, relinquished mind and bathing body - here we are, burning, hoping.

The boys are going to do it: chase the new karma, head up North, hati hati, push push - here is your dream, here is your divine thunder, thankfully beyond the skinny material attractions and hammering words; beyond the cool and the time; beyond the momentary shine, the elegant meanderings of lie and greed, the heavy weights of gold and diamond, the rising cost of blood and land; the boys are hiking up the hill to Dharamsala, wiry and free, possessed by a new glory, a new shinning light; hopeful in their smiles, Godly in their wanton silence and bonded love; up the rocky roads and clouded peak tops, across the carved bridges, endlessly imbued.

They smile at the passing children, who stare at them from the cobble roadside trenches, who offer them rice and water and flowers as they pass, with a giggle and a greeting - hello mister! they yell; lightly, unsure of the outcome, their invite, the way - hello mister! you are are going to see the guru yes? please take these beads, and these scrolls.

Sure the winds are good, sure the waves are heavy, but the boys are chasing temples and Nirvana at a higher altitude; a beauty, a heartbreaker, never attainable. Confident in the early evening, their spiritual host guides them up the stairs and into their sparse quarters, with a wood slat bed and a bucket of water; a round cushion to sit on. On the wall is a chalk drawing of the sun, large, with jagged mountain peaks in the foreground, yet there is no sound of ocean, no smell of sand, just a strong ray of light through the window, and the gentle vibrations of a spiritual home (another spiritual home).

They sit and breath all day.

They repeat mantras and roll mala beads.

They see lights and colors and family and silence.

They lose themselves fully and find someone new and unfamiliar. They don't talk, they don't write.

They read the scrolls and smile at passing strangers.

They fast for the early days and have visions of soul and God, then they return to themselves, and every time they envision putting their heads through a brick wall, because its all energy, so they do it, and smile.

Then the guru smiles, secluded in his study, surrounded by books and journals and elephants and mandalas and pencils.

The boys walk around the fountains and across the ridges and along the dirt path through gardens of tulips and roses, and wander blissfully, aimless, through Redwood groves, up and down crumbling stairwells that all rise to gorgeous simple towers that look out on the valleys and across the clouds.

The boys nod at each other. Dressed in twin robes now, they

remember each other, but wonder what has happened? With every passing day a greater gulf of enlightened madness, a further adventure into the murky black holes of self and being.

You came all the way for this! The Voice bellows to them both in the night. You've come all the way for this – now here you are, the same and fantastically different, elevated and fabulously basic – rich and smothered in mud, without gold coins or flimsily bills; you've come all this way, sat empty and divine, here heroic in worship and sacrifice, beautiful and wholly original; all this way, grateful and humble.

Now go back, The Voice proclaims. Mercilessly be yourselves.

How do you think the swell is? Henry asks.
Pretty good I'd imagine, Mr Heavy says.
Waves of your life, Henry says.
Perhaps....... Mr Heavy softly replies.

Awake:

Outside a nightclub in North Vietnam the bar owner pulls a knife on Rooster.

You are stealing my customers! he yells. You work for Violet! he accuses.

He pulls out a long blade, at the end of a smooth ivory handle, in a dimly lit parking lot, crowded by junky scooters and high end Japanese road bikes.

You steal my customers now you pay! the Owners says.

He takes a step closer to Rooster, his bare feet bruised and dirty. His smoke stained white shirt only partially tucked in, and his black slacks torn at the right knee, and cut short above the ankles.

Rooster is a foreigner, on holiday, visiting his dying father in an exotic land, with no money and few language skills, clothed in his own rags, without a shower or a shave for three days, living on heartbreak and cheap beer, praying for his father, caught in another jungle, clouded in judgement, divine in intention.

Rooster starts his bike and yanks a young American prom queen onto the back.

You work for Violet! the Vietnamese man hollers. He races towards the bike, dull blade shining and arms wildly reaching.

Rooster revs the engine and launches the bike forward, narrowly passing through a crowded car park, up the ramp and out onto the street, immediately assaulted by the weaving lunacy of traffic.

He reaches his hand back and touches the prom queen's upper thigh, jelly and smooth. He smiles as she kisses his neck, and nibbles on his ear.

For the love or the money? Thats the haunting question, the total deluge, the epic concern - battles for the heart and the soul, the sand between the toes, the element of adrenaline and fear. Living, that premium which boldly accompanies all the elevated endeavors concerning water and human, light and dark.

The camp roars for a bit then settles again.

A mission is cooked up, and the The Saphos get stoked. The bikes start up, the boards broken out, the winds light yet steady, the swell just starting to come in.

A little place in the sun, just at the jungles heavy edge, quietly wedged between the ocean and the hills, safely planted away from Malibu and Coolangata – perhaps early Oahu, perhaps mid way down the rainbow. Its very peaceful, very airy. The angle of the beach, luscious along the large sheltered bay, south of the long seaward points in time, with sun and the fabulously spinning earth placed perfectly at the islands jeweled painted feet.

They say that Gerry would sit out the back and wait for ages, patient, silent, a Zen man, radiant, levitating, then pull in swift and clean, and never look back.

Plans (less is more). Penetrating, up to no good, searching and screaming and entirely independent of prejudice and concern.

Without the weight, never having to say no. The beach is open, free (for now), and powerful. Always bring the love.

One young Australian, out solo in the midday sun, further becoming one with IT; (whatever you are), (wait, you know.....); the emotional trials of overpopulation, expensive cities and surfy pink styles – of flashbulbs and square pieces of foam that Ryan Birch certified, made famous, recycled, and called cool.

"If you're a puss then you're a puss, no matter where in the world you are."

The Safos bring the funk, the monster mash, the money money. The Safos sit around looking at photos in the AM.

"I like Parko," he says, confident as time, beaten and strong.

The tide is coming up, the bros laugh and get stoked. Billy Corgan plays, a cut to the face, a lounge before the storm, again hati hati, again wild. Raptured in red, part way to liberty, to water, in the dull sun lit mornings, cool and easy, breaking days, offshore and incredible.

The power – hello peace, hello world – you crazy behemoth, you dancing song, twangy siren. The monolith, the exotic cause of self destruction, the allure of rant and spice. Dream, a little rain, a little accident. Take to the bow, elevate the temples, breath against the damp grass and hollow hide – young warrior, ballroom darling, uptown hustler, curious snake; where is the swell? the boys ask, looking out at the ocean from the main house, watching the light slowly spread across the clear early morning sky.

A few small waves come in, clean yet confused. The power is still obvious, yet reserved. The blanket of energy, the raw savage spirit of inherent freedom and boundless ability – stand up, walk across the earth, unstoppable. Feel that hue, the immense palate, that destructive allure – the fetish, wet and crying, lost between fear and childish curiosity – beaming with perseverance, hearty and empty, ready to plow into the fresh morning break.

The classic cause, the imminent rift between work and love

– meet me on the beach at sunset, and whisper me your dirty desires and burning secrets; your castles in the sand, your long cold showers and empty beds. A fierce decent into spectator, while she prances into the room, and smiles, and bounces away with a slim dark haired stranger and all his gold.

The pirates decide to wait, full on bare and gristle, absolute and ferocious – watch her, remember her, dream her, lovers that arise, in the desolate shade of night, in the honest moments, in places far way and new. Strange, the little tea cups and boorish exposures to light; the amorous fields of gravy and wax. That is all you need, that is all you've come for. This poetic babble only howls the grinding soul, and scares away the girls.

The aces, the madmen, the hellions, charging in the early morning, free of place and ache – the machine is far away, the alarms have all been silenced. It takes a certain breed, Henry realizes. A memorable action. Wonder, music, chance.

Get in there, Henry says to himself, watching the wave out front, unsure at times, blatant at other times. The older boys get out there early and enjoy the quiet open space and desolate company that the island offers. The time creeps along, lazy, with a slight chill in the air – a quiet living, a match made in heaven. More spray across the back, easy at the lip; simply honest, simply beautiful. The fun, all out and blind to the calls, the blinking ambulance sirens, the heeding of death and malnutrition – seemingly aloof, yet ready to go.

When poetry was sexy, Henry ponders. Brilliant, hopeful. When young girls swooned and went wet at the swells of verse. When the great world ailment diluted in song. When the fruit was fresh and the water clean, living in kings time, in this century, in this house. The restless soul celebrates Shakespeare and Lopez, the astral days lay brick and dirt at the base of Mount Sumatra.

Aye, you endlessly wondering where it all went: the empty pockets and pangs of bliss. Aye, you lay out by the beach in the clean open air, and dream of mountains and ocean, and be thankful, and watch the waves break, just a few meters offshore.

The Captain comes down from the tree house and grabs the gun from off the surf couch. He smiles. A crooked devious unpredictable grin, and turns to walk lightly back to the tree house, a perch above the main peak.

He rests the gun in a corner; an empty room, save for The Captain, a log book, and the gun. A pack of cigareetes and a glass of fresh mango juice sits on the wooden desk in the middle of the room, with The Captain seated squarly behind it.

From his seat he can see out onto the camp, and out to sea; he can view the boat come and go, the surfers paddling in and out, the guests on the veranda of the main house, and the staff shuffling in and out of the large open dining room, in front of the closed kitchen.

The Captain, in his worn board shorts and brittle skin, his intentional head nod and bloody moods. The Captain, alone now in the jungle, with just a sly grin and a deed to the land. A devilish commitment to an island that constantly tries to kill him. He hums to himself, a tune from the boats, a tune that the young men used to sing when they arrived at a strange port, excited and willing, prepared to embark upon a wild evening of woman and song. So he hums the tune, and allows the old lovers and dirty towns to visit his memory, then quickly clears it all out, with a salty gruff and a stomp of the foot against the freshly cut wood floor.

The Captain looks out at the camp. What have I done? he silently wonders.

The boys stand in the board shop and sand off the resin from the nose of a clean white surfboard, shaped like a race car, with the name of a small town local shaper along the rail.

Michelangelo works with a single sheet of sand paper, shuffling his feet slightly as he presses hard against the foam board, careful and precise, chipping away at the resin, gentle with his fingers, firm with the palm of his hand on top of the gritty paper.

Do you think the trip is worth it? the short Scandinavian man asks tentatively.

Sure, the wind is perfect for it, Michelangelo replies.

And do you think they will head out on the boat? he asks.

Yes, the wind is straight offshore, which is good for there.

Sure hope they get some good waves, the Scandinavian man says. His pasty white chin and chubby head is curiously memorable. He is easy in the afternoon doldrums, slow and purposeful around the camp. The other guests have fully retreated from the sun and heat, seeking solace in their nameless bamboo bungalows

They deserve it, Michelangelo says.

He stands back from the board and looks at his work. Not yet, he thinks, then steps forward again and resumes his work.

Its a very nice place, the Scandinavian says. I should like to return here someday, when I am better suited for the conditions.

You are doing just fine, Michelangelo reassures him, honestly, with confidence, believing.

Yes, but I know what I am capable of, and this trip has just been a bit of what I want, a preview for where I want to be.

Its a nice place to be, Michelangelo says softly.

The Scandinavian man smiles, knowing the implication, letting it pass.

Yes, you are right, he replies slowly, and forces a thin smile.

Michelangelo returns the smile.

We have all been there, Michelangelo says lightly.

He lifts up the surfboard and examines his handy work. Smooth, clean, sturdy. He passes the surfboard to the Scandinavian.

Here, he says flatly. Try this for a sword.

The freedom is deadly, like a kiss.

The Captain watches them paddle out to the boat, all five of them, with colorful surfboards beneath their bodies, over the rips and out the channel. A small single outboard engine boat waits just beyond the breaking waves. The surfers each have red dry bags dragging behind them. The Captain looks at this watch, then back to the ship, at the two young crewmen under the boats protective canopy. They casually lean against the boats front driving console, watching the approaching cargo. The dense hungry jungle spreads luxuriously behind them. The boys chat easily, and point at The Captain's treehouse, then look northward, up the beach, at a set of breaking waves, and they agree that the small waves here are a good omen for their trip.

A bit of swell, The Captain thinks. He sees the miles and the money; the gold and the cheer. Keep them happy, he told the boys. Without them we are all homeless and broke.

At night they eat well. Rice with a combination of lightly spiced vegetable: potatoes and carrots, string beans, cauliflower that has a spicy curry flavor to them, and tofu stuffed with cabbage and shredded slices of carrots. Clay pitchers of fresh water and tea, along with glass carafes of cool red wine, are all spread out neatly, properly spaced, on the food bar outside of the kitchen wall.

A young local boy stands at each end of the bar, eagerly ready to refill empty pitchers or seek out any random requests from The Captain and his guests. The cutlery bares The Captain's family crest, in a diamond shape, freshly polished and neatly stacked, separated by purpose, together with intension.

Always clean, always proper, The Captain tells his staff.

The Captain paces around the dining room. The sturdy feel of dry land remains unusual under his feet. Even after the war, and the injury, and the hearings; the wives and the detractors, the blood and the heartbreak; all this time, and still he always feels the gentle rocking, the reassuring instability, never fully acclimated to this steady dirt and stable wood.

He passes slowly through the dining room and looks at the precise placement of flatware and cutlery. He eagerly searches for the irregularities, and basks in the high performance.

When we succeed we are kings, he tells the boys. Let them

never go home dejected and beaten. I've raised you all to be great, he tells them. It is a simple service, he says. Now plainly do what is asked of you, and the allusive shield of peace and happiness will visit you often.

At the table he is quiet, while the guests tell stories of the days adventures: waves ridden, places seen, jokes heard. The men burst with celebrity and privilege, while the boys eat in the kitchen, quietly, as the local women sort through dishes and clean up from dinners long preparation. Their eyes are clear and their jaws are firm.

Thought i was going to die, one of the men says.

Fastest drop I've ever made, another man says.

Best waves of the trip, a third fair skinned man admits.

The Captain drinks heavily and smiles. His eyes dart calmly from face to face, as he studies the lines in their skin, the character in their jaw, the worries in their brow, the love in their eyes.

I know these men, The Captain thinks to himself. They were me, many years ago, before I came here.

The men verbally joust with each other. Sarcastic, playful, familiar.

You are a crazy bastard! one says loudly, and they all laugh in unison.

Henry paddles over the first wave, and eyes the second. Bigger, fuller, rising up and full. He decides against it, paddles over the lip, goes airborne, and lands in the trough with a familiar, loving clap. He raises his head, and sees the third wave of the set: clean, empty, glassy, with two visible shoulders and a peaking center. He leans back on his colorful 7.6, spins around, and paddles with full commitment towards land, as the waves rises behind him, then under him.

Henry pops up calmly, turning his board casually to the left, high on the wave, and drops down, with all the speed he can maintain, and glides along the face, harmoniously, without concern, viewing the lip above his head, pulling into the wave, then back out, down into the flat, then back up again; dancing, celebrating, mellow, as the section in front of him closes, and he points his board at the lip and goes airborne again, over the top, and down onto the other side.

Good morning dreams, goodbye envy.

The rain makes everyone tired.

Look at that left! Rooster says.

Sore, beaten, cut, again alive in the far north, with the water buffalos and the sharks and the vibrant jungle leaves.

Made it through, Henry thinks, clambering up from bed. Made it through, now here we go again. Lunatic days, tempestuous night, poetic shine, infinite joy – ahhhh! The Gods have granted me the terms of all colors, all facets of nature, all believable tails and shapes of lady and wine; the sea has blessed me daily, kept me safe and warm, well fed and sane, and now as the rain falls and the waves crash and the camp begins to stir, an ode to this ridiculous living, to this fairy tale at the oceans serrated edge.

Henry pearls over the nose, makes another airport pick up, plans another novel.

The local girls smile and purse their thin lips.

Learning them Western ways, Rooster observes. Dangerous to us all, he continues. Fun, until her daddy comes down here with a machete and takes that pretty boy American head clean off.

In the city they caught a man trying to steal a motor bike, Rooster continues. So they beat him with rocks and hammers, poured petrol over him, then set him ablaze in the middle of town, in front of an angry mob of locals.

What do you consider savage now? The Captain serendipitously asks.

In the car park a small group of men in tattered clothes gather around a small video phone and watch the glowing screen flash images of a man getting his head cut off with a dull knife. The men in the parking lot laugh and point, together, bound by the horror, amused at the brutal reality, convinced of purpose. They laugh deeply. Everyone wonders.

The Saphos sit out in the sun, awash in morning heroics, glory, snapping close up photos of recent reef scrapes: shallow cuts across the mid left buttox cheek, a long scrape on the shoulder, a bloody spot on the forearm. They drink juice and water and eat noodles and eggs, with sliced tomatoes and cucumbers in hot sauce, frothing for waves and adventure, all day long.

To a man with a hammer, everything looks like a nail.

The Captain stares out at the sea, hypnotized, with lists prodding through his head: waves and dollar signs, a few things more..... The open blue sky, the metronome of responsibility and love, as another squal moves in, and the boys joyously all exit on motorbikes to chase swells. Yet the troubles still bounce around The Captain's head, even with the beach so quiet.

When one starts mixing candy and razorblades. When all the land looks valuable, and the ocean shines like gold. When the clouds are for sale, and the earth is on the block. Grabbing grabbing..... Believers, beautiful, survival - the path to excess - hati hati you hear, in the shadows, in the triumph and the defeats. Failing to act foolish, being an adult before its overated punching bloody time.

Elegant, pushing, more, treated as a star; moody, top dollar; a mad man and his hotel in the sun. A poem on the radio plays, soft and slow. The fraternity, the Pequod, the front room and the view out front, all quiet, finally.

Rooster makes coffee. The Captain does the numbers. The photos get snapped. The Saphos are out in the water. The kitchen is quiet and the winds blow offshore. The sky is a shameful grey, with hints of blue. The big days are yet to come. The young fools scramble for gold, and the podiums, and the bright lights.

Ask her for naked photos, Henry thinks. Her thick lips, her wobbly thighs, and the scarred wrist. Brutal, blessed, the waist line; the hip, the eyes, the tattoos and the jaw; the needle marks and the heart. Tell her you are coming to see here, Henry plots. Someday, later, when this is all over.

The boys sit around the dinning room, as saints, with souls of diamond and fire, hearts of platinum, and sharp tongues. The boys march to the sea, then wait in the shade, while the tides rise and fall.

What we need is love, Mr Heavy loudly sings, as the wave sets come roaring in, clean and long. Heroic again, the mystic beauty, the dirty sheets, the honey tunes and smiling eyes. Bring me the water buffaloes, give away the gold, he thinks to himself.

Just a bunch of nails, just a bunch of motherfuckers, Mr Heavy casually tells Henry.

A mosquito net house, the long dark hours of night, the deepest slumbers while the boys continue to drink beers and tell stories: the girls, the piss, the nights out in Singapore, the beatings.

There is still swell in the water – the sun comes up slowly.

Amazed. Heavy – thats the call sign.

The Captain sits next to the group of young boys and listens quietly. He laughs, smiles, smokes a cigarette with an air of high aristocracy. Drinks his brandy slowly, disgusted by the haste.

Going slow is much faster, he tells them.

The boys dart around the table, yell over each other, pound back the cans of cheap beer, and laugh psychotically, awash in the salt water air and the evening freedom.

No one orders, no urban noises sounds. No car alarms and sirens, no traffic lights and anger.

Tell me the one about Angela the Bush, one boy says. Tell us about the red head assassin from North Dublin.

How did you get up here Captain? the boys ask.

Love and glory, The Captain replies.

Long way from home Captain, another confirms.

Always, he says.

The Captain eases into his wicker chair, the cushion of his seat thinning with time, and smiles wide, free of regret and wonder.

In the darkness they look towards the beach, the ocean, the star filled horizon, and they laugh, and they wonder.

The silence creeps in suddenly, and The Captain rises from the table. He walks into the kitchen. He greets the evening staff with a smile. They are washing the nights dishes and storing leftover food. One girl is on the ground sorting dried orange peels.

The Captain pours himself another brandy, feels the warmth of the liquid fill the cool glass as he cups his hands around the rim. He exhales deeply.

Damn kids, he thinks to himself, paralyzed in the bright kitchen, suddenly anxious under the pelting lights inside the house.

He turns and exits the kitchen through the twin swinging bamboo doors, and stands outside in the empty parlor room. He looks through the open bay doors of the parlor room, out to the veranda where the boys continue to laugh and tell stories. He looks past them to the ocean in the near distance, the heavy sounds and battling moods, longing for her touch. He turns and exits through the side door, and he walks to his cabin, gracefully, with the brandy swirling in his glass. He watches the ground carefully as he walks, sure not to step on any cobras in the night.

The life of the harpooner, he whispers. The early morning take. Burning, along the sea, the sailors know the time. Always crashing, the beast, the antidote.

The scribe, the hero; the time in the water, in the soul; wild.

The winds lighten up and turn. Its a difficult place to forecast. Always the siren of multiple swells in the water, always the looming squalls. Always swell, rarely perfect.

Its the latitude, Rooster says. A little further north and its would be sheltered, a little further south and it would be flat. But we are here.

We are here.

The ocean lumps up and closes. Chops and obliterates. The new swell is messy out front.

Mr Heavy is drinking in protest, the rest are in the water.

Watch and learn, the timing is everything, Heavy thinks.

All you've got. All you.......stripped down, weary, without the clean legs, without the million dollar lip; the thousand dollar glance, the miracle. Here comes the chop again, here arrives the saints. Everything that has happened, everything that will happen......a pacing group of nails, the finest authority in local meteorology - from behind the mast, the tattoos, the grease and groan.

If she sends more dirty pictures then you go to California for sure, Henry tells himself.

You drown in those arms, thin and tan, void of the bubble - the selfish regard and shallow concern, the mast and board and tea - you sleep for days in that bed, in seclusion, and then astounded by how peaceful you feel. If you can make it around the bend, be a magnet, be kind and simple - a throaty laugh, a genuine countenance and flail, in the giant puddles, and swirl in the evening air, and dance in the open fields - a star, a milky way, a rainbow. If you can skip across the galaxy with a guitar string and a good book, magnificent, as the heat pounds and the merchants sit quiet - the poppy head promises, the major dialogues between giants, the abandonment of kings, the glory of the blade; into battle again! as the beast, as the heart.

Groovy, Mr Heavy sighs, unchained and wild.

The sharp tenderness of ability, from 68 feet up on a wave. Above the reef, as a legend, a connection, a shy genius; and all the heroics, no longer in the dark, always spread out, in serious wonder; the stacked sky of clouds, the shades of water and grains of sand; they call for rebellion, and a cool million dollars to insure its real. Henry reads about the legends, and gainfully ignores his sullen personal legacy.

The Captain walks in - a Zen orchestra, invisible, manic, personified, motherfucker and rage, explode and disappear. The island, here, cranking. The fresh tears of realization, the whispers of heartbreak; and the sirens ask you to continue, unburdened, stripped, as a child, as a mate. The brief honest smile, the work to keep you sane.

The Captain looks out at the ocean.

A couple of waves, he says. A bit of work.

Jimi Hendrix plays, the water buffaloes cross the front yard. The sun shines; sama sama – the ahimsa routine, the elephant in the room.

A dagger at the heart, a looseness to the soul. Ishmael with a low wave count, the heroes in the lounge.

The saints go to sleep, the moonlight is beautiful.

GETTING FAT IN SUMBAWA

*

1.

it's hot already – the way, the motion, all moving, barely ready – where are we going? where is the final destination? how did we get here?

i'm gonna get fat in Sumbawa, she says. she takes another healthy spoon full of peanut butter in the waiting lounge, drops another orange peel on the ground.

fuck it's hot – spinning wheel, up all night – the dj dropped James Brown at 1am so we had to stay, he tells her.

sacrilege, just above sea level – dedicated to granola and tempe; dedicated to water and fast girls; break it a bit more, watch her walk out, make it funky – what's my name? what's my motherfucking name?

damn, what's up cuz, how you livin holmes? the voices persist.

everybody wanders around in open toed sandals, wasted, hungry, trolling, anchored next to the dj, glued to the bar, glancing at the ocean, making out with a stranger, promising the future to friends, hard up for cash and table manners; nothing is the same, everywhere is crowded, everyone is beautiful.

we are all assholes, she laments.

we are all God, he tells her.

Lightning Bolts and Disco Girls

a fast affair, a brief seance, a two tone pair of shoes and tiny white walled tires for the Vario scooter parked up the hill; (avoid the crowds, watch out flavor, goodbye celebrity), opened up late night, just pulled in.

hope you score, Buddha says, and they lock hands, catch eyes, and are momentarily sincere, forever caught, running running running.

you as well, Henry tells him, and then it's over – back to the combat.

2.

they bring Paul Newman warm beer and meat, in the shade, and that's all anyone wants, with the shore close by and the television loud, the flies hover and prey – practice practice practice.

respect the Gods! and the water, and the green. he hears the voices.

There is less plastic, less waste here, Henry thinks to himself.

absent the garbage along the road sides, the candy wrappers and stray bottle caps; the playrooms of cigarette butts and incessant traffic lights. further from home, further from the bright lights – somewhere under the omnipresent Hollywood sign (it's everywhere).

the girls are singing, the trees lightly sway, as the sun boldly pelts the roadside, the burnt empty pastures, the historic rice field representations, the looming volcanoes, the mocking sea.

hati hati, again and again.

Brussel Sprout hooks up the tunes, clumsy and helpful, while Paul Newman shuffles through the jukebox, slips in a nickel, and searches for the dub tunes, the hard shot, the boogie boogie.

spicy and free, out of the bubble, goodbye matrix, hello groovy; a 5 cent party by the ocean, with a sway and a fist pump – tap that foot, snap them thumbs, over and over again, with a head nod and a money train cache.

GETTING FAT IN SUMBAWA

its sexy time, Lana Del Ray, warm Bintangs, veggie nasi champur, and the young girl who runs the joint blushes blood red and pretends to watch the television, but really she digs into the boys, the heroes, the divas, and the dancing water fools.

i'm a Go Pro the fuck out of you!

Paul Newman gets some Dixieland going, spins the best tracks for the empty warung girls and the dirty water beach envy angels. Brussel Sprout lays down and catches some z's on the cold hard marble floor, on her back, straight, with a clean pink and grey sarong wrapped around her short tan legs to keep the Muslim boys wondering.

its a girl! its a girl! the Muses scream, and everyone wonders how big the swell will actually get.

solid, twice a day, and clean - a dream, a new menstrual cycle. the younger chicks cant make the plane for the islands.

better I do not come, she says. stay safe.

thanks beautiful, see you in a couple of days, Henry tells her, and means it. lightly injected, between the hari cari, on clean sheets and moaning.

Bintangs with ice and orange juice for Paul. water for all the third eye virgins, with spicy nasi champur and meat satay that gets the boys going. all 70's groovy, all mellow. classic rock and roll plays from a small round mobile speaker the size of half a brick. pass out its so hot.

Henry disappears, Brussel Sprout keeps her promise, and Paul Newman chats with the driver in the high afternoon sun.

its not California, he explains. its not Hebrew School.

heavy house music all the way across Lombok. Henry wonders if this is the first time Danny Tenaglia has been played here.

the local kids stare out from under the shaded street side stalls, crack the minimalist smile, the hard tropical greeting, as Henry bobs his head and shoots back a samurai smile.

"whats up brotha» he says at an intersection. «we are all one."

Because you turn me / you turn me on.......

the music plays steady.

everything takes an hour – resolved. at night the road windes and twists up and around a small mountain. a new freshly paved road, wide and dark, without any light except the stars, plentiful in the dark evening sky, without shopping mall lights and Taladega Avenue strippers.

when you get out there it sounds like a war, Einstein told him.

the drivers turns left at a non descriptive corner, slows, and stops. a young boy in tight stained blue jeans and a T-shirt with a large photograph of Biggie Smalls across the front, briskly walks over to the drivers side window. he hands the driver a fistful of blue fifty thousand Rupiah notes, and walks away in a dull silence.

a broken road, old and tattered, with sharp potholes and random dips in the worn away pavement, into gravel and light brown dirt, with empty fields on either side of the car, and tall tropical trees looming over the sharp curves and steep straight aways.

Ketut drives in silence, intensely focused, and Paul Newman hacks up flem and spits out the open window. Brussel Sprout is strangely serene, with her window half open and the fresh warm evening air ventilating the back seat.

its warmer here, Paul says.

yes, Henry replies.

this place has a wonderful feel to it it, Paul Newman adds. foreign and quiet, he says.

peaceful, Henry observes.

silence.

i am hungry, Brussel Sprout tells the car. how far?

not long, Paul tells her.

how long, Ketut? he asks the driver.

close close, Ketut says.

the road deteriorates, the night sets in, the malaria is touch and go. the allusive freedom is contagious, addictive, weird.

hold out, Henry thinks. breath deeply. a ginger chest and a

chocolate mantra. he dreams about the morning, in that fresh chlorophyl way, and her mysterious bite.

style and function. he painfully wonders. welcome to fat in Sumbawa.

3.

I'm only twenty five, but I look thirty five, Ernest Hemingway boasts.

how old is she? he asks Henry

about twenty two, Henry tells him.

to old for me, Ernest says mournfully.

I've been in the jungle for a little while ya know – starts to get weird, he says.

they laugh, eat fast, drink the ginger, gaze hungrily at the waves out front – everyone waits for the winds to switch, for the tide to drain out, for conditions to improve. the bondage at breakfast shimmies across the dining room, and all the water addicts mull around in the dirt and sand, awaiting glory and imminent heartbreak.

she will kill you, Paul Newman tells Henry. right as rain. sure as sunshine. and if I preach to you all night then maybe you will get some of this pirate wisdom into that ugly brick head of yours. but I doubt it. just like I doubt she will make you happy. just as I doubt you would know what to do with a ton of happiness and a room full of girls. bloody useless mate. but have no fear – those sleepless nights are just beginning.

Henry sinks into his hard wooden chair and surveys the horizon. the jungle all around, the muscle beach transplants and Ferrari steam machines anchored along the sand.

he smiles, exhales deeply – you motherfucker, you bitch, he thinks to himself. all your ancient wisdom and daily psalms, broken with a hint of chilly wind and destitute milk. can't we simply settle into a long term tantric agreement, with the lights off and the kettle boiling; the traffic all stopped and the silence

Lightning Bolts and Disco Girls

pervasive. the beating heat like a crack in the jaw. the hopes and prayers and rugged mountain side dreams, just a flickering moment in the ongoing span of thirty lifetimes. maybe more.

the fool and the lifeguard sashe out to the beach and surf Third Grade, at a high tide.

what a sense of humor the universe has, Henry realizes. what a stabbing significant other she must be.

wish you were here, that is what the photograph says. just make me famous and you can fuck me for another five years. that is what Henry thinks Brussel Sprout says.

laid out on the grass under the heavy noon sun, a drip dry romance, a knife at the imminent homicidal orgy. the tide drops out a bit. ginger tea and pumpkin bread in the dining room.

the madmen, the bipolar Ernest Hemingway water victims, all on the down low, in the quiet afternoon, when Brussel Sprout puts on some tunes and the whole beach exhales with a love song – into the trenches again my son!

the void is a motherfucker. the irony is a crossroads, all waving back.

you should surf a single fin, Henry tells her, walking back up the beach, sinking into the soft white sand.

the dry desert cliffs rise up to the east, and the turqoise dream ocean opens fully to the West.

why? Brussel Sprout asks.

because a beautiful girl surfing a big single fin long board is the coolest thing ever, Henry tells her.

its not about being cool, she says rebelliously.

its all about being cool, Henry says. unsteady, unsure, with no where left to go.

along the beach in wet silence the rocks crumble and the sand winks an eye at her kinky dysfunction and autonomous mind fucking.

you see those yellow flowers? Brussel Sprout asks.

yeah, Henry says.

very pretty, she says absently.

Paul Newman plays the banjo and Brussel Sprout rolls up the cigarettes for all the broken devotee bastards. the heavens sing:

Baby please don't go / baby please don't go / baby please don't go, down to New Orleans / you know i love you so / baby please don't go.

Henry whips up the ginger and sinks into a corner, breaking the mirrors and victim to the clock. Hemingway is shirtless, eating rubbery pineapple pancakes and worrying about the government.

been out here a little while, Hemingway continues. been lovely, lonely, without her dangerous touch, sharp as a heart attack, that reef is.

the boys all fall in love and never paddle out again. the girls promise happiness and revenge – no more history, no more worry.

Paul Newman hits a high note and snaps a string, as the legends get ready for another day on the throne, and the booty shaking hip hop girls pass the time in a dirty kitchen, boiling water and preparing dry nasi goreng for the soldiers and their enflamed bursting beachside bellies.

play something slow and sexy, Brussel Sprout requests. play it like you love me.

Newman plays the bottom two strings and eases into a slow, drowning, burnt and bruised rendition of Folsom Prison Blues, with June Carter on one shoulder and Vietnam on the other.

play it for *me,* Brussel Sprout orders, halfway through the last verse, and Paul Newman explodes into a sad Nagasaki voice that makes the trees cry and the beach sand swoon.

don't call me anymore! Brussel Sprout yells to the swaying dining room. dont promise me another star, from your hard pants and drowning soul. dont be an asshole. dont miss me anymore.

the music plays a little slower, the bass wild and allusive. Brussel Sprout creates another diamond, and flashes her Marlene Dietrich smile, from up high.

pirates and celestial vessels in the Memory Motel, paying cheap rent to the Buddha house maids and the whispering ex lovers without a home. playing the guitar alone in a red Chevy Nova, pretending to not be lost, to not be wanting. tough, the two hour work day, the paradise castaways, the dregs of temptation and swine.

love me a little more Brussel Sprout demands. you spineless weeping motherfucker. don't cum so fast! she orders.

nobody asks what she wants because everyone is scared to hear the boiling answer and bleeding response.

Say lord, lord lord lord......mmmmmmhhhhmmmm......

4.

all you take, all you give – the fresh morning breeze, the easy sunshine, the master stretch and empty breaking, deep and deep and deep – remember that beauty and style, that memorable goody goody chant:

AUM.......

here we go again, speaking cheese and sucking on peanut butter while the tides keep changing. Buddha Buddha, beauty beauty, free at last, free at last – touched and instrumental, the ocean is a pinball machine, no one can find Waylon.

Brussel Sprout rock and rolls in with a head lamp shining, a small fish at the end of a spear gun, with a happy grin and a moonshine strut.

been out past the reef, she says, all wet and dripping, with all the pirates looking hungry and bloody.

mushi mushi, she says with a smile.

respect the Gods, and you can all saunter back to my place for ginger tea and a fresh case of heartbreak.

the pirates laugh and grin, show off the latest wounds, discuss the daily drop ins, the tumultuous Brazos and Youtube hype breaks. the bullhorn pans to the elder statesman.

when I was here in 83 we surfed it with just three people in the water, The Legend says. wind was perfect, 6-8 feet, sunshine and groovy.

his yellow silver hair, cut just below the ears, trim and strong, slightly hunched over, displays a lifetime in the water, a sea destitute devil, paddling between foreign continents, leaving another love, chasing another swell, for reasons housed in mystery and obscure purpose.

we anchored just off the coast, in a channel, he continues. stayed there for a week, with perfect waves and no one else out.

say lord, lord lord lord......

Brussel Sprout laments the deep sea failures while Paul Newman rolls another cigarette, and Hemingway watches a short surfing video on his oversized black brick laptop computer. the dinning room rises and falls, a Caribbean color paint job sets the mood – turquoise, yellow and red – and the beach is dark and mischievous, just across from the aching palm tree gardens.

I was so close! she says. right in front of the fish. but when i went to shoot they all swam away so quickly. I missed every time.

less killing, more orgasms, Henry says to her. follow the signs and simply believe.

she looks at him hard. another round without a smile. Paul lowers his head and contemplates his eternal silence and three day celibacy trip.

it was quite scary, she reveals. we saw sharks, and some puffy fish that came very close to me, then swam away again, twice! I tried to shoot it, but i missed.......

Henry tries to remember why he invited her.

she asked Henry 'what should I bring?' in an empty cafe along a busy street.

a big surfboard, a pack of ginger, and a jar of peanut butter, he told her.

I'm going to get fat in Sumbawa, she said

you are the rain and a fresh mountain flower, Henry told her.

oh, shut up, she says flatly.

Lightning Bolts and Disco Girls

5.

a heavy, beastly, Mae West on steroids, crackhead serrated glass motherfucker of a wave.

Paul Newman takes the first thumper of the set, following a long paddle out, and he looks good from the line up, but inside he goes head first straight down.

Earnest Hemingway sits deep and waits patiently. he has been around the hood for years, looks like your average southern hemisphere hooligan, but delineates the bullshit like a prodigy.

he makes a couple of long tubes before the Happy Mean Boat Dudes get lined up. he surprises the celestial judges, a doubtful poetic style that scars the pretty girls but attracts all the angels.

he paddles back out and sits wide while the current sucks all the bra bra boys deep and inside. The wave breaks further outside, on the larger sets, and dances across the reef tall and mighty; so rough around the edges, so young and ragged, still free and wild, without the ache of fame, self conscious monologues and celebrity expectations. she is fast and hollow, marching with the same old technology, demanding sounder equipment, greater courage, egregious efficiency - up all night making the butter, churning with the Sunset Boulevard dreamers and the Fresno tweekers; the fantasy corners and cheap blow jobs; the serrated lip and refrigerator barrels (my life in the tube, by Edward Abbey, or.....); all punchy and freshly worn, Jesus on a good day, Sonny Liston on a tear up in Vegas, sucking water off the back of a young Daytona stripper, pissing gasoline into a handful of sunshine.

the soundtrack plays a dark muffled Hendrix for a serial killer fix, and the house wives take off their dripping panties and welcome daddy back home.

been here long enough, Hemingway says. should have my timing down by now.

lets go out to the reef and fuck all day, Brussel Sprout whispers to Henry. maybe you'll get your balls back.

call me Charley, promise me the moon.

6.

Brussel Sprout walks in with a spear gun and a smile, wet with water, the preferred Sumbawa butterfly, the big time motherfucker. the local survivor kitten puts a deep red hole in the backs of every unsuspecting water boy. the boats release the hostiles. into the trenches once again my brothers! they yell.

spit back ancients psalms of grease and waxed lightening, puts the hammerheads up at the point and pray that the winds switch by tomorrow – tidak papa – hold down the cape and spit out the homophobes, its going to be a Saturday night boogie woogie freak freak show. someday, with an easy breeze, enough to keep the sun behind a colorless wall of clouds, disappeared, remote, the taste of salt water, on everything, pricing the slideshow by the kilo, wondering what tomorrow might bring.

tuned out and sandy, even the crazy Brazo got himself a big titty sweetheart down at the beach.

Brussel Sprout stands dripping and warm by the lotus tree, staring at nothing but a dream, and she says I'm bored again..... the feel of ocean and blood fresh on her skin, and she skips back to bungalow number four and masturbates in the shower to the sounds of Krishna Das and the raw jungle get down.

soon we go home, she reveals. back to the traffic and the strobe lights. back to the text messages and local hati hati grind machine.

do you dig my perspective? she asks. do you groove on my homicide?

bring back the 57 Chevy! Paul Newman announces. reinstate the draft!

Everyone is a legend around here.......

Henry Castle and Paul Newman walk down a dusty side road that goes into town, and watch the clouds move fast and slightly grey across the late afternoon sky.

someday this will all be strip malls, Henry muses.
someday we'll all be gone, Paul confesses.

Lightning Bolts and Disco Girls

they pass a young Peruvian kid with a deep tan, a short board and no shirt on. he walks past quickly, and lowers his head without a smile.

friendly kid, Paul observes sarcastically.

fucking surfers! Henry rails. if he ain't gonna smile at us then who's he gonna smile at? a couple of bankers? an accountant? he thinks its all just barrels and pussy. he doesn't get how big this thing is - how communal it is - a comrade, a brother. fuck....

used to be that you passed a car with a surfboard on the roof and you both stopped and chatted about where the surf was good, Henry continues. what boards you are riding, where the good music is at. now you pass with your head down and hope no one follows you..... my wave.....what are you fucking crazy! damn kids gonna fuck this up real good. goddamn spoiled criminals with a short board, thinks its all just water.

Neil Young is God, all the girls are beautiful, all the waves are perfect, and all the dudes are cool. ram ram sita ram, sita ram sita ram, ram ram sita ram.......

at dinner Earnest Hemingway grabs the young Peruvian boy by the tight collar of his white t-shirt and turns him hard into a wall. he screams directly into his soul.

you fool! Hemingway says. don't you know its not about you! its about us all, and all the gold, and all the sunshine, and all this water, and all this beauty, and if you destroy it - if you kill it - then you will kill them, and you will kill me, and you will waste away, without soul or purpose or love.

fucking useless children, he continues. and if you try my heart, in this action, in this sacred place, then i will rise up with daggers and poison from my gentle wet blind liar and live to crush you as well. and then we have war, and what good will you do to me and it do to you? asa fragment of humanity, as a tiny lecture of transcendent prayer, as a single fin aficionado on the inside without weight. what then, of you and me and them and this place? what then......? you motherfucker.

the boy melts into the safety of his distant riches.

smile you scared motherfucker! Hemingway demands. if you kill all this then you will be no better off along this lovely road alone. for we are all alone. we are all suffering. and we are all lost. so pull into me and believe, for a single kiss from her is equal to a lifetime of waves; and someday, in our ashen state, we will remember only her, and the taste of salt, and the peaceful feeling of warm morning sunshine on our burnt treasonous backs.

Brussel Sprout pretends to blush.

so don't tell me of life and death and indecision and hope and envy, Hemingway continues. the frail Peruvian boy, still lifted to his toes and still pined to the colorful wall.

don't speak to me of pain and glory and failure; don't compare this to that and back talk the Gods. don't bring around the winds and the beat and the baby blue skies. its just us here, just us in it. you and me. you motherfucker, you fool, you selfish angel; you wandering savant, you dancing Buddha. we are the same, we are all one.

now go out there and stop being such an asshole. and pull in more. and smile broader. and believe more. and trust it all. then surely they will all love you, and all your perilous dreams will come true.

7.

Brussel Sprout settles in and orders two scoops of ice cream in a large white porcelain dish. the couch is a pimp baby blue, and she sinks in, sighs, takes a spoon full of mint chocolate chip with caramel syrup and a thick whip cream. she mixes it all together in the dish, grunts and puts the spoon squarely into her mouth, above the tongue, and closes her lips around the silver handle, and inhales. she feels the cold overcome her warm, dirtied, tired body. the airport lights make her nauseous and dizzy. her comrades stand around the ice cream display case, wondering what to order.

fucking madmen, she says to herself. damn children.

Lightning Bolts and Disco Girls

Henry Castle and Paul Newman decide on the different flavors: cookies and cream with english toffee vanilla, and fudge chocolate brownie with strawberry cheesecake.

in the mirror they look scruffy and handsome, the image of beguiling cowboys and silk road carpet dealers. the rugged misfit kind of men that rich urban women dream of yet never choose. with their open shirts and untrimmed facial hair, under their uncombed manes and over their aching bodies.

this is great ice cream, Brussel Sprout says. we are lucky to be here.

Henry and Paul Newman each grunt and trade spoonfuls of fast melting dairy from each others pools of sugar.

damn hippie! Newman says suddenly.

God save the queen! Henry playfully replies.

if this were Beirut we'd all be in pieces, Paul Newman says. and this gun street girl here would be traded for goats and heavy blocks of gold.

Brussel Sprout smiles through a mouthful of chocolate, caked along the thin curve of her upper lip. she bows her head and shuffles her body a bit along the seat of the baby blue booth, simulating a lazy curtsy, while the boys polish off the imported ice cream and sway to the faint sounds of Earth Wind and Fire, oddly played over the terminal PA system.

we could have been stars, Brussel Sprout says.

we could have been heroes, Paul Newman adds.

we could have made sandwiches and called our mothers, Henry finalizes, with a wide catwalk grin and pocket full of hundreds.

with the lights back on and the tables empty, from one bed to another, wrapped in young virgin lovers and past life deficiencies, they go.

mix in a little sugar, add that grinding salt, hanging steady above a sharp reef, that gives fine tongue and hits up all the gentleman for cash. from the mountain top Earnest Hemingway is hollering in the rain, naked at Supersucks, masturbating for

the Irish.
 tidak apa, motherfuckers!
 fool. the girls are all out and dancing, the golden years are here again.

MADRID

*

it has been two weeks since I've been with a women, he says. wait, let me see.....

there is silence while Raphael counts the days on his fingers. just the sound of ocean and night.

yes, two weeks, he continues. in Madrid. she was amazing. not the best. i cannot say the best, because I've had the best, and, well, um, she was not the best. but close. very very close.

Raphael Fortuna and Henry Castle sit across from each other and sip their respective noodle soups, with tired bodies. sore. silently relieved.

you know, here, i do not eat any meat, Raphael says. his Spanish accent is sharp and drawn out.

i am like a vegetable, he continues. no meat. but soon. yes, soon i will have to eat some meat. soon or my body will kill me.

he clamps his right hand around his long neck and dramatically squeezes.

there is a tratoria on the way to town, he continues. is that how you say it in english? tratoria? yes, there is a tratoria on the way to town. you know it?

on the left side of the road, Henry quietly answers.

yes. that is right. tomorrow i will count my money and maybe go there. but only if there is enough money. but not for a pizza.

Lightning Bolts and Disco Girls

no pizza. for some pasta! oh, what i would love for some pasta - some macaroni pasta. ahhh! yes. some spaghetti bolognasia!

the boys continue to eat in silence. the soup is hot. simple. made from plain packaged noodles, then lightly spiced with pepper and salt. fully processed. cheap. momentarily soothing. they add hot sauce, from a dirty glass bottle, to enhance the taste. make it deeper. international. fill the body, they think. anything. starved. dry. depleted. done.

the sun is already down. in winter it becomes dark so early. the night opens up suddenly, but nothing of priority now for the boys. no plans. the tide is out, the beach is quiet. in a few shanty guest houses along the cliff there is music, and dimly glowing lights. the sound of German and French being spoken in the distance. the laughing local boys, full and honest. a women's soft voice. a chime.

the waves sound smaller, a young man's voice says, from the descending the stairs.

today was enough, another voice replies.

the boys sit still and listen in silence. they ingest the simple foreignness of the small village, and alluring ocean.

what is big enough for you then? Raphael asks Henry.

Henry shares with him a brief memory: a giant shadow along the horizon, blocking out the span of the earth. is this death marching towards me? Henry wondered. will this truly be the end of it all? the body cannot handle more water like this. you paddle for the outside, Henry recalls, with everything you have. your life is in the balance, you think. but if you keep thinking, you will have less strength, Henry concludes. if you have less strength you will not make it over the horizon. 'there is nothing to worry about.' Henry keeps repeating this phrase. this is the mantra. survival, second by second. a rare blend of nirvana and absolut hell. the dream.....Henry wonders. of course everything is going to be ok.......

i am a struggling elitist, Henry says with a faint smile. Raphael

MADRID

offers him a bemused look.

at the cliff top men and women gather to view the early evening heroics. the sun casually slides below the distant horizon. again wild displays of oranges, pinks and blues. beneath them the bay is being torn apart by waves and rip currents. the ocean is furious. long rows of bubbling white foam, as high as houses, erupts along the outer reef, when the waves thunderously crash.

a nameless blonde boy, lanky and tan, riding a fat red and yellow painted surfboard, stands out beautifully amongst the crowded line up of surfers. he takes a steep drop, then rises back up the face, and shoots out forward, carefully, ahead of the closing wave. quickly. casual. Henry remembers that: a tiny red ball wrapped inside a barrel of water, speeding down the line. other boys are getting washed up and destroyed further inside. Henry remembers that as well.

don't let me die here, Henry tells himself. elsewhere, closer to home, but not here.

it is the food that i miss the most, Raphael says exuberantly. yes, the food.

in my country we have great food, he continues. like in Italy they have great Italian food, and in France they have great French food, and in Germany they have sausage. in my country we have great food as well. ham and potatoes, and all the beautiful fishes.

he smiles broadly, triumphantly, transported for a moment.

what do you have in America that is American food? he asks. maybe hamburgers, he wonders.

french fries, Henry laments sharply. but those are from Belgium, i think.

right. so you have every kind of food but none of your own, Raphael concludes. very strange.

maybe, Henry softly says. but we have fried chicken and collard greens though, he adds. apple pie and cotton candy. coka cola and snickers bars.

they finish their spicy noodle soup in silence, and think about waves, and girls, and food. the small village is already silent, and half asleep. there are many stars out, but the two boys are seated deep under a high thatched roof, and can only see out to sea. on the lower horizon there are no stars. it is dark. the lights from town dimly shine in the northern distance, a world away.

today i went to the beach to look at girls, Raphael later says. i am very attracted to women now. it has been two weeks since Madrid, and i feel it. like a bomb inside of me. so i went to the beach and just looked at the girls. my sunglasses were pulled down over my eyes, so no one can see me. ha! such a pervert, he laughs. but they are so beautiful there at this beach. oh my, what a beach! he says, as if in a dream.

all the Brazilians go there, Henry carefully points out.

they must, Raphael agrees. there was this one girl! you know, she wore this thin bikini, that came right up her backside, like this........

Raphael cuts through the air with his fingers, drawing a coarse diagram.

very tiny. very thin, he says. she was in the water alone, and i just watched her from the beach, behind my dark sunglasses, wondering......

she was surfing? Henry asks.

yes, but not serious, Raphael answers. she paddled out, and she talks with some of the guys, and then she paddles back in after 15 minutes.

hmm, Henry moans.

yes, so lovely! Raphael exclaims. i just watched her play in the water. i cannot surf myself, because all the time i am just watching her. when she got out of the water i could go catch waves. but not while she was there. she was very distracting to me.

exhaustion hits Henry suddenly. he sinks deeper into his hard wooden chair, and slumps over his bare arms, folded across the small round table. if there is any other place to be in this world then we may have gone there, he thinks to himself. but this must be the place, because we find ourselves here, with nothing to do, but surf and go to the beach, and that is everything, and that is enough. enough for a lifetime, he silently concludes. enough punishment to be good at something.

he closes his eyes and thinks of home, of long ago, then pushes the memories away, and lifts his weary head off the worn wooden table.

they walk down along the beach to François' cafe. there is no crowd tonight. no women. most are asleep already.

a healthy looking older Moroccan man, wearing yellow and red polka dotted black beach shorts, sits at the end of a weary wooden bench and plays a gold faded acoustic guitar to an empty audience. a young local boy sits opposite him, and accompanies the guitar on a pair of knee high bongo drums. they play slow and sad, but they are both smiling, wild and free.

the boys casually nod towards the band, familiarly, with a knowing smile, and continue walking across the outside patio.

François is behind the bar, dancing alone, drinking red wine out of a short plastic cup.

this wine comes from a dirty box! he confidently exclaims.

He welcomes them with his deeply drawn French accent and evening growl, and continues dancing lightly, in a crowded space behind the small bar, under a bare single ceiling light.

this is the apocalypse, Henry says to Raphael.

Raphael smiles, but does not understand. he regrets walking down to the beach now.

after dinner it is good to walk, Henry confidently tells him. it stretches out the body, and reminds you briefly that there is more to the world.

it feels very late, Raphael surmises. but it is not.

the boys chat with François for a short time. about France, and Spain, and music.

François is freshly shaven tonight. his face is gaunt and thin. a clean sunken face and a tan malnourished body slithers gracefully behind the faded white counter top. he is forever sun soaked; disowned, under appreciated, completely free and happy. He smiles often, and wide, and reveals his two missing front teeth. the boys smile with delight, and love their vaudevillian night charade.

this is why we are here, Henry says to himself.

they laugh fully, and endure it all.

you come tomorrow, François tells the boys adamantly. we will play chess, he resolves. there will be girls, he assures them. after all your silly waves, he wisely concludes.

the boys nod obediently. they smile honestly, with appreciation. they are warmed by the invitations, the music, the warm glow of the single light from behind the bar, the momentary assurance in it all.

we needed this, Henry thinks to himself.

we will return, Henry says assuredly to Francious. tonight we are weak from the sea. we are wandering as if in a dream, he says. lost and alone, even while we are in the illuminating company of others. damn pirates and youthful delinquents. damn beasts.

yes, Raphael cautiously agrees.

we have no where else to go, Henry admits. we have nothing else to be.

good, then you will find it easy to be here, François concludes. tonight and tomorrow, perhaps always. if you win, or maybe if you lose. nobody really knows.

Raphael Fortunana and Henry Castle stand in the middle of the cafe and let the wisdom sink in. we know nothing, they think in unison. we are so into something......

the boys thank François for his hospitality. the musicians have silently snuck off. Looking for girls and wine.

the boys carefully descend the short steps down to the beach. they walk along the damp sand in silence, without haste, inevitably returning to the hard empty stone stairwell that will lead them to their barren rooms and hard beds. the beach is dark and empty. the guest houses line the cliff above them. there sleep

MADRID

the wasted bodies and lonely hearts. lions and daggers.

they stagger forward, between the sand and rock, feeling the hard and soft elements across their sunken ankles, letting their gaze soften to the night sky, barely seeing the waves breaking a short distance out to sea, hoping not to cut their sore bare feet on the sharp dry reef, and scattered sea shells.

the best time ever, Henry thinks to himself, and smiles, in the deep evening darkness, far from home.

Lightning Bolts and Disco Girls

S H A Y

*

An empty ocean, she moves easily through; the sounds, alive, while gazing at the handsome water, infinite; and the dull clear blue of a new mornings sky......paradise.

A chill in the air, a bit of suspense. With the tide so high the waves are unpredictable. The ocean is waiting. She is putting on her face. There is no rushing. She drifts from the mirror to the bed, then back to the mirror. There is no telling what might happen, it is still a dream, where anything remains possible. A lightening bolt as a compass, a drip of salt water as a map.

Shay is beautiful. Striking. Raw.

The beach has successfuly consumed her. The grains of sand, the hardened reef, the rocks along the shore, consumate with her clear white skin, burrow between the folds of her sunburnt concioussness.

Surfboards and tan bare skin peppers the immediate tropical landscape.

She remains impervious to the madness. For a little time. Her jungle style wisps past the third world shanty style Warungs along the beach; past the newly arrived pale skinned sweethearts, sunning on the clean white sand; and the drunken surfer boys, lost under the tantric sun and unforgiving moonlight. Shay moves deliberately around them. An unpredictable affect. A spontaneous bargain.

The tattoo on her ankle is a star.

You eat some of this, she says.

She puts a plate of freshly cut pineapple slices in front of his deeply tanned face. Twenty thin slices, from a small pinapple she has been peeling with a dull butcher knife.

It is not ripe yet, she tells him roughly. You can see that. But it will taste fine.

She smiles at him, in a familiar way, that suggests they may have been lovers for a long time previously.

He briefly hesitates, then leans forward, and takes the plain white porcelain plate filled with fruit.

She is beautiful, he thinks to himself. There are pieces of gold and silver jewelry in her nose and lip. A bold statement. He is attracted to her sad, wild air of chaos and destruction.

Tastes wonderful, he says lightly.

Of course it does, she replies. That is what I said.

She smiles again. She winks at him, steps towards him, and speaks in a low, unrefined voice.

The rest of them snicker, she says. They say it is out of season. But they are French snobs, and do not know any better. You and I will eat the pineapple and be happy, while they remain sour and sick.

She places the plate with the full un cut pinaple on the table in front of him, and cooly walks away. He watches her the whole time.

As she walks her body easily swishes from side to side. A ragged denim mini skirt hangs low on her narrow hips. A thick brown leather belt sits loosely around her swaying waist. Her faded black T-shirt is purposely torn at the arms, and made into a loose fitting tang top. There are cut slits across the back of her shirt, allowing her silky bare skin to shine through.

Shay attracts attention, as she glides effortlessly across the main patio of the Cafe Leon, from the open kitchen to the small uncrowded bar, under the palm trees, next to the clear blue ocean.

The wave was good this morning, Leopold says proudly. I go out this morning and it was good. But so many people...... he commiserates.

Leopold points to the clean breaking wave in front of the beach. Perfect liquid lines extend across the horizon, radical and blue, rearing up, then running the length of a sun burnt sky.

Good, but so many people.....Leopold says again. Maybe next time I take my gun out there, and then less people.

Leopold proudly points to a spear gun laying in front of them, on the old wooden sun bleached table, nestled tightly along the rails of a creaking wooden deck, over looking the beach and the crashing sea.

So many people.......he continues. I hate the people you know. It is true. But i love them, you know.......but in the water, I hate the people. It is very strange, but you know.........

His Italian accent meticulously bumps over the English landscape, while his hands dance across the thick warm air.

Henry and Leopold stand on the terrace of an old rotting guesthouse, on the north end of the small beach, and contemplate the sea.

A swell has come in, and the waves are noticably bigger then yesterday. Under the intensity of a strong afternoon sun there is a full line up of surfers in the water. The line up has been full all morning. They launch themselves into a fast left breaking wave, and glide heroicly across a clean tubular face.

One young local boy launches into the air, over the thick lip of the wave, and lands in the flat ocean just above the reef, behind a continuously rolling mass of salt water.

The girls are lined up agreably in the sand. Little gangs of beauty. They watch the surfers from clean towels, adorned in new tight fitting bathing suits, shining red and white and yellow. Their designer sunglasses mask any desires that their eyes may reveal, while their hats are appropriatly slanted. All day they lazily wait in the sand, while their momentary lovers – admirers, suitors, prisoners – are out in the ocean, being stars.

They sit casually, with matching stern looks of indifference. They have attained a complete understanding of this cosmopolitan beach way, and are finely adept at how to be successfuly wanted. All these miles to be pretty; all these miles to be fabulous, that is what their body language says. There are few better ways to be fabulous, it is rumored, then to arrive here, at this local white sand beach, far from home, anchored in the middle of a foreign ocean, and act like nothing matters. Take it or leave it, their indifferent frowns reveal. Does not matter any longer.

They reveal no dramatic looks of surprise, no hints of awe. Even with the parade of superheroes out front, pulling into 6-10 foot waves, there is no break in the stone perfection of their professionally chiseled, solemn faces.

This is how it simply is, their expression's say. We have studied at the best beaches, in the South of France, Western America, The Gold Coast, and The Hamptons. Their perfected bored stares, across a long stretch of sand, the tanning angels, forgotten misfits, are endlessly fortunate, and govern the beach.

Shay sits at the bar and scrolls through the text messages on her cellular telephone. She is serious now, sitting with a surprisingly straight posture, her tan brow fured, her thin red lips strained tightly together, pulling her small curved chin up into her concerned face.

Have you met my friend Henri? François asks her.

She absently looks up from her phone. Shay tilts her head to the side, and examines Henry for a moment. His tired body, his loose fitting wrinkled clothing The deep tan of his skin, the ample dirt and sand under his cracked finger nails, and

SHAY

between his sliced toes.

A hard, empty, yearning look from his dark brown eyes stare back at her in blank surprise; tough and confident, yet unsure of this new woman,

No, she smiles. Not yet. As she properly extends her hand, Shay tilts her head to the side, and considers his desheveled frame again. Another wandering pirate, she says to herself. Another lunatic.

Henry Castle, he says soflty, introducing himself properly. He takes her hand gently in his, squeezing slightly, feeling her thin elegant fingers flat inside his crude white hand.

Shay, she says smoothly.

A pleasure, Henry says.

Yes, she says curtly, and slowly pulls her hand away from his.

She nods slightly, instigates a momentary connection, then returns to her telephone.

At the bar François is lightly dancing to the soft Caribean music coming from a single old wooden speaker placed on top of the stained white refrigerator. He drinks beer fresh from an old cooler under the bar, cold, with ice water still dripping from the bottle, as he methodicaly dispatches the beer into his tiny frame, and gets drunk.

Annabelle watches him and smiles. She sways to the music, and adoringly touches François's cheek with her left hand. He smiles, leans in close to her ear, and whispers dirty words in French to her. She laughs fully, with age and wisdom, and pushes him away.

You are drunk, she tells him affectionately.

I am in love, he professes.

Ah, such a hard worker! she says.

They dance around each other, gently touching, then instinctively letting go, in practiced time, until the song ends, leaving only the sound of the taunting ocean and playful night.

He is impossible, Shay says. Exhausted and disappointed.

Lightning Bolts and Disco Girls

What is wrong my darling? Anabelle asks her. Why so much trouble tonight?

Anabelle cups her soft wrinkled hands around Shay's angry fists, and squeezes. .

There is lightness here tonight, Anabelle instructs. We are all in love here.

He is impossible, Shay repeats vehemently.

Of course he is, Anabelle tells her. And you are crazy. That is the way it is supposed to be. That is why you want him.

He is the one insane, not me! Shay says sternly. She attempts a rightious display of self assuredness, her eyes damp and dark, with thick black mascara gently thinning under her dangerous green eyes

Of course he is, Anabelle agrees. We are all insane.

You should forget that pimp of an American and spend time with my friend Henri, François interjects.

François places his palms on top of the two womens hands, and rubs his fingers back and forth on top them.

Or come with me, he continues slyly. You know that I am the best lover on the beach.

The two women laugh and smile.

It is true! Annabelle admits. But you have slept with all the women on the beach! she says exuberantly.

They laugh again. The two women lock eyes, momentarily curious, then continue laughing.

Henri, François pleads, they are so angry because I am good at what i do. Is that not crazy? If I were a great astrounaught they would not be angry at me. They would give me a medal and money. But here, for being such a great lover, I am shamed, and treated like a peasant. For what? Only I have had the courage to reach for what I truly desired. Only I have been so sweat to these two amazing women. One who has sworn herself off of men like a witch, and the other who is in love with a pimp. Why I even allow them into my Cafe is a mystery……

SHAY

François winks at Henry, and smiles mischeviously. His thin aging face is tan and slightly wrinkled. Decades of unadulterated sunshine and infinite sand have worn him into a practiced tramp, a melancholy poet. His clear blue eyes are sunk deeply into his thin face. His forehead is shallow and serious. He retains the handsome looks of an aging film star, from a previous generation, when the screens shone in black and white, and were mysteriously silent. His narrow jaw line exits directly at his thick pink lips, forever wrapped around a bent and burning cigarrete.

Here Henri, he directs, waving his hands towards the open space at the bar. You speak with my darling Shay. With honesty, love, and arrogance. Then she will no longer be heart broken over her American pimp, whom we are all so jeleaous of.

Shay smiles innocently at the attention. The silver jewelry on her face is distracting. Her skin is deeply tan. Her short black hair is curly and unkept, yet the thick dark strands rest appropriately in place. Henry wonders to himself if she has labored hard to obtain such a look of destitution and defilement, or is it natural? Women are paying hundreds of dollars at salons all over the world to make them look wild and dangerous, yet she manages to achieve that allusive freedom with much less effort.

She stands alone at the bar, leans back a little onto her bare heels, lowers her chin, then dives directy into Henry.

You are American? Shay asks.

Yes, Henry replies with a broad smile.

So why should I love you and not my American pimp? she asks quickly, as if suddenly she has little time for these intruding evening theatrics.

Because I am honest, Henry responds flatly.

Ha! she laughs curtly.

Anabelle and François are dancing again behind the bar. They weave in and out of each others arms, with lazy, happy expressions across their faces. This is the night, their faces say.

Lightning Bolts and Disco Girls

We've nothing else to do.

Already you lie to me, Shay tells Henry. That is not the best way to be my friend.

After a pause, Henry ventures boldly.

Who said i wanted to be your friend? he asks deeply.

Shay smiles suggestively.

Of course you want to be my friend. All men want to be my friend.

Perhaps I am not like all men.

She giggles.

Henri, you are funny, Shays says. That is good. To be funny is to be kind. But you are all the same, all of you men. You want me to sleep only with you, while you act like a hungry dog chasing all the girls on the beach, and repeatidly fuck all the easy young tramps on the Penninsula. Then you are surprised and angy when I come crying to you at night, with a broken heart and rancid expectations, and try to kill you in your sleep.

Henry stares at her, gauging her honesty, unexpected and alluring.

You've never tired to kill me, Henry replies slowly.

We have just met Henri, Shay snaps. Do not try to be smart with me.

She lights a thin brown cigarette with a cheap lighter that reads Chicago across the side, and quickly blows the smoke over her shoulder.

Intelligence is over rated, she tells Henry. Better that you look good, and have manners. That is all a women really wants.

They sit in silence now, and stare at each other, with similiarly determined expressions of love and destruction.

You are magnificent, Henry tells her directly.

I know, Shay replies.

Henri! François screams suddenly. Come over here, and me help with the music.

The boys watch the ocean in weary silence, and wonder where to surf in the afternoon. Where are the waves best? they repeatidly ask each other. Where are there no crowds? they lament.

It is a circus out there, Raphael says. He is fed up with the crowds and the hustling. Even with all the beautiful girls on the beach, and the warm water, and clean waves so close, he is exasperated with the daily afflictions of hunger and greed.

Yes, Leopold agrees reluctantly. But the wave is very good.

Yes, Henry sighs, weary of the sun and the travel. That is true.

The sun has burnt through the early morning cloud cover, and relentlessly attacks the beach. The boys stand in the friendly shade of a shanty Warung, at the foot of a cracking ancient stone stairwell, and meditate further on the ocean.

This is the end of the world, Henry thinks to himself. This is absolute armegedon.

Another non descript boy launches down the face of the wave. Too deep this time, he fails to make the opening section, and is immediately swallowed by the wave's hungry face. He disappears under a cloud of exploding white foam and churning water, and the boys wince in unspoken solidarity.

It sounds like a war out there, Leopold says flatly.

The waves attack the reef relentlessly.

After a permited silence, Raphael asks Henry if he will see Shay again. He uses her name, as if physically familiar with her.

It is best not to speak of her, Henry says flatly.

Why not? Leopold asks sharply. She is only a girl, he exclaims. Please do not confuse her with some mysterious black magic, or dangerous curse.

Maybe....Henry manages slowly, unconvinced.

They return to their standing silence, eager for the dance, yet unsure of the partner.

A young local boy launches off the lip of a wave, and spins

through the air. A foreigner with blond hair beats out a hungry line up of men and pulls into a large barrel, deftly manages the drop, casually disapears behind a wall of thick salt water, then exits successfuly, up and over the lip, so he is not sucked down onto the razor sharp reef.

Voices from the beach cheer and scream. There is an energy of enthusiasm. A surprising erruption of love, appreciation, and inevitable madness.

It is like this every week, Henry thinks to himself. The wave capital of my tiny world. The hungry beach, the starving line up, the endless passing of my precious time. The oldest of stars have fated me here again, he silently wonders to himself. Into the water – into just this.

They watch the waves for awhile longer. They surrender to the inevitable, eventually. They gather their equipment silently, and quietly participate in the slow walk down the stairs, and into the ocean.

SHAY

Lightning Bolts and Disco Girls

BEAUTIFUL DECISIONS, HEROIC CHOICES

*

*

Greg Alman

little the poets remember; great the time.

my sunset honey, my dead lover – in memory of Elizabeth Reed, chicken and waffles at François's......fabulous.

a bit deeper – rest in peace – mama I'm a rock and roll star; mama I'm on a roll. 1973, feel that breeze.....easy sugar, that mess around; you so shy, California you getting it now. sexy pleasantries – always clean. vigorous, heavy; the kid has her humor and her tattooed mama – now thats love – now thats style.

good evening Mr Allman; paradise 101.

74, The Beacon Theater, with two Jersey girls and empty pockets, splitting a bottle of hot water, charmed by the lights. little foot tap, little Cadillac mama, with the greens, and the string bikini starlets, all up in pink, all shiny for that cool kid in the canvas shoes and the purple fedora; listen to him play brotha! an apostle. a hanging jump shot. here we go, its candy cane smiles and single beach girls, all weekend long.

i know what you need, Henry tells her. and she just smiles, because she got it, and he wants it. gambling for that sunshine touch and evening lover - its all comes around, and she knows it....

on my way to New Orleans this morning......

pinch pinch, nickel nickel, let that jam go, let that honey take her top off; its all barefoot and bad mama jama - all water and disco.

you write about love? she asks softly.

fucking into love, then back to fucking, he sternly replies. just like living, just like a broken champion.

the sun peaks out, the Spanish girls strut up and down the beach; stern faces and angel hips. send me to the factories, Henry thinks. once more to the bone yards.

my lover is on the way, she tells him hesitantly. better not get comfortable.

I'm a napalm bomb baby! Garbanzo confides; with a hint of love and the fresh taste of white walled tires.

Henry walks up the beach for a shot of turmeric and a foreign sweetheart without a name.

best to just call me development, she introduces herself.

best to label me hate, Henry replies.

all morning the sound of water, all night the smell of sin. specializing in purpose and pontificating - all the young men are doing it.....best to take the blues, then the pinks, Brussel Sprout tells him. you never know when its going to come up; you never know whom she might speak with next.

on the dance floor she shuffles from one suitor to the next, innocently smiling, displaying enough skin to keep the crowds interested. she sips from a small water bottle and promises them all the world. Henry picks the flower pedals and watches the butterflies bounce.

Home again, he tells himself, in the shallow corners, next to the empty beer crates, just on the other side of the speakers. she loves me, she loves me not....

no more sex with women I like, Garbanzo firmly reasons. only passing fancies and obvious disdain.

a hopeless romantic, Paul Newman confides.

a motherfucker, Henry concludes.

its a bloody mess, Brussel Sprout adds. and you fumbling bastards have no idea about love and service.

perhaps, Leopold tells her. but we are all dying in style.....

Henry ducks into a beach side cafe and practices being a warrior. I'm the new harpooner! Hemingway proclaims from the bar. I'm the new butterfly tamer.

at this point the wave starts to break, an indication of the week ahead, a prayer to Veruna.

make me a humble man, Henry says. with a mean backhand. make me a cherry picking two step savant. gone deep, letting the sunshine do her thing.

1974 in the sand – we are a blues band, we are a gypsy love affair.

the merchants are head hunting. i like what orange does, I've left Wall Street for good.

This is where the revolution is, Garbanzo surmises. this is where we march. the sand and her spirit, the ocean and her love. its never what you think – its never easy.....funky and smiling, dirty and pretty; smile a lot, he hears The Gods whisper.

oh lord i feel like im dying......

hi mama, nice to meet you.

feel the breeze, forget the time; long haired and sexy, blonde and beautiful. play me those dreams, turn off them lights.

cause in the end, the love you take, is equal to the love you make.

an orange shot of mischief, a long stretch of ocean to calm the spirit. she picks up and carries all the weight, maneuvers all the heartbreak. Greg Allman leans back and lets the revival go. back to Highway 1, back to the machine. elevated and free – no problems honey, no hassles. as the tour bus pulls away, as the tide slowly drains out.

*

Diner

the sound of you, below the rock, above the sand, with honey and style. remember: dark night and sunshine, regret and redemption; share the stage, wake up with the sun. action, time, the bellowing rooftop pirates, the soothing cool air, the clear sky, the airplanes constant in the distance. they are dancing above the cliff, they are tempestuous and bouncing. free, breaking, worn, revitalized. the couples dine together on the beach, the candles flicker in the evening air. we discuss the day, the waves, the ocean, the sunsets, the music. we sway with the tides; made, saints, motherfuckers, aware, and gone. simply a peaceful corner of the earth, an oasis in the sand. no hurt, no hate; no anger, no envy. the Gods are smiling again, the stars are shuffling past. no more building, no more senseless development. home – far away and gone; the fabulous city lights, the greatest show on earth.... you take the universe, you take the kisses; the time, the money; you light up quickly, go dark with the epitaphs and the wedding vows. pour me another cup of honey, hassle me another taxi cab.

just be peaceful, The Gods say. just be heroic.

hati hati – fresh from the Indian Ocean, adoringly committed. don't know nothing else – have less regard for consequence. saturated, peaceful, smiling; the picture cool, the mountaintop, the beach; gentle salt water, dear stranger, passing women, dynamite technician, high heeled lover; am perched upon the star, circling the sun, burning for you, and the tube, and the heart. better with a slow smile and a mellow walk – better with the lights out and the opera on. games the game; get closer to it, feel the cool breeze, silent, as the hours pass and the water rises. the dining tables slowly empty, the beauties go passing by. the prayers go out, the kings off to bed, the butterflies fall in love, again. again.

been curious, been a brick house. made to dance alone, made

to hear the music. am full, unknown, magnanimous; simply here, ensconced and dreaming in full. tucked away in the corner, melancholy with the night, easy with the choices; where ever you go, how ever you are, making the babies with dark strangers, accepting the harpooners fate. pirate first, fire soon after. a wild mess of adoration, obsession, perfectly in tune, easy on the eyes; another evening magic, another long days work. the gratitude and her wild wild wonderful beach children, waiting to go outside, because it feels so good there.

*

Morning

healthy, happy, simple – my sunshine delight, my morning star. as the breezes roll in, as the planes sound, off in the distance. she just lays there, awash in water and soul, taking in the dancing horizon, breathing below the waves; a gentle look to the south, a treatment, as pitch and grace colide – simply here, she confides, clearing away my concerns.

warm, delightful, quiet, ancient; the orb of light and bliss visit for a moment, to wash away the theories, the hardness; as you crawl along the sand, dive into the blue, participate in the parade. morning darling, nightingale on the cliff, devil on a curve; empty the pockets, dig into the day.

*

Freedom Is Sexy

we sit here stranded, but we're all doing our best to deny it.
tell me, she whispers. be honest.

from the moment i saw you, from the first touch. all the boys know, all the stars have their pull. its better when we fuck, he tells her. simple. sincere.

Lightning Bolts and Disco Girls

yes, she replies. don't worry.

the sky parts, the lights go off, the drip drip, the honey honey.

here we go, he tells her; now lean back, inhale, arch, believe. its just me, it's not the first time.

she checks the locks with her eye, beads of sweat in her palms. what are you worried about? she asks.

nothing, he replies.

worried i'll get attached?

yes.

worried i'll show up on the beach everyday, follow you around? look at you intensely from the other side of the room?

yes, i'm worried about that, he answers.

worried i will call you. i will email you. i will come to your house.

none of that, he says sternly. he squeezes her nipple, hard, and she moans, and he twists a bit more.

no emails, he tells her. none of that.

she smiles through the pain.

just fucking, he tells her.

he watches her. the twist in her neck, the wrinkles beside the eyes, the bend in the nose, the thin Chicago lips and cock sucking jaw.

just fucking, he tells her again. he inserts two fingers inside her.

say it, he tells her. just fucking. let me hear you say it.

she smiles, slanted, arches her back, rolls slightly onto her left side, bends her knees, clenches her eyes shut, and licks her lips voraciously.

you fucking whore, she tells him.

and you love it, he replies.

go with love, he hears the voices say, and he does.

not so fast, she says sweetly. we have a whole lifetime to discover each other.

he burrows his head into her stomach, rolls his tongue around her belly button, then continues further down, along the curve of her waist. he feels the cool silver button of her faded jean shorts on his chin. he shakes her loose, then dives in deeper again; engaged, osmosis, divine.

she giggles, lets out a sudden sigh – a moan, a deep inhalation; she rolls onto her hip, curling her legs underneath her body with a long shiver.

gently, she orders.

inside you, all of you, he tells her. mine now, he says.

she laughs, then goes serious. her eyes deeply focused on him – all of him. she wonders how serious he is. what his angle is; his pedigree, his charms, she quickly considers them all.

you've gotten further with me then most, she admits to him. you've no idea what i am capable of.

show me, he tells her slow.

not yet, she replies.

he opens her legs suddenly, and gazes firmly between her thighs. he hovers above her, prepared, silent.

she smiles fully.

what do you want? she asks. he delivers a thin cryptic smile.

i want you, he tells her. tonight, tomorrow, and after. for a fuck, for a love, for a friend. i want you, and everything you have. your skin. your taste. your moan. your lips. your wetness. your anger. all your primal jealousy, all your medieval charms. i want to fuck you, never see you again, then fuck you again. i want you to think of me all day; to wait for me, to long for these hands between your thighs, moving freely inside you. let me see your lips, but never kiss them. love me deeply, and fear the wild danger, the unknown losses and insidious positions.

i want you and all you are, he continues, and lowers his head between her thighs, and softly runs his tongue along her smooth white skin, from the small of the hip to the knee cap, then back again. civilized in the madness. an animal and a gentlemen.

she reclines and looks up at the dark black sky and the silver shining stars. confident, isn't he, she thinks to herself. a problem, a gift, and certainly trouble.

another shiver rises up in her, from the pit of her stomach, the recess, between her dark wet legs and her flat belly button. the shiver crawls across her body, under the skin, perfect, incorrigible.

don't change a thing, she thinks to herself. he will make you cum all night.

and i said you love me? and she said yes, i love you. and i asked can i stay? and she said no, you cannot stay. and i said its because you love me that i cannot stay. and she said yes, it because i love you that you cannot stay.

just listen to that beautiful break, to that unreasonable charm. he reckons its all going to happen again. that its going to keep happening, over and over again, until they both destroy each other; until they both change.

the sound gets deeper in him: calm, sensible, content. just a moment, sharing the love, humble before The Gods.

in the morning he watches Juji put the flower trays on top of the rock, with the incense sticks and the pink rose pedals inside. Juji places the trays carefully between the moist coral rock. he steadies them on a slight angle, then steps back, places his palms together at the center of his chest, lowers his chin so the center of his forehead touches his fingertips, and presents his morning offering to The Gods, in silent communion.

Juji turns and walks back up the beach. peaceful. he stops, bends over, and picks up a coconut husk that has washed ashore with the high tide. he flings the husk further up the beach, where the sand gently meets the cliff walls.

do you love me? she asks again.
yes, he replies.
silly boy, she tells him.
yes, he says. always my problem.

she walks down the beach and sits in the sand, away from the crowds. the ocean water lightly crawls over the exposed reef, not far from her seat. she crosses her legs and makes her back straight. she tucks her chin into her chest, closes her eyes and breathes deeply.

at first she counts her breath – inhale, one; exhale, two. she repeats in this way for a few minute, until the sound of her breath becomes more interesting then the counting. the numbers slowly pass away. with her eyes closed she sees images of her son, of her lovers, of her husband; of the passing boys on the beach, then the ocean and a burning crimson red sunset. there are quick flashes of light and a sprint of energy, like a lightning bolt, clean and fresh, three times, across her eyelids, across her forehead, into her third eye, penetrating; then a calm haze, an orb of light, floating, simple, empty, consuming.

he stands still, a short distance away, and curiously watches her. he takes a few steps towards her, then stops again. he squats down, takes a handful of sand with his fingers, and lets the grains slip out from his dry palms.

beautiful he thinks. silent, confused, trying. every dream, every open door, and he just wants to hold her, a little longer, and touch her skin, and kiss her waistline, and dig his fingers deeply into the curved crease of her hip; to stay there for hours, he considers: my unavoidable lover, my inevitable heartbreak.

she opens her eyes sharply, and sees him there, close and silent, smiling now. inquisitive, watching her softly, adoringly. she feels him, *then* sees him. the colors all mix together. suddenly.

i need more time alone, she snaps.

he smiles wider. stretched clenched lips. he nods his shaggy head, slowly rebellious yet obedient. done. broken.

ok, he replies.

he stands strong, full, no longer wondering, and turns back north, up the beach. he walks casually along the dark bare reef, sharp and cool under the firey setting sun.

do you love me? he hears that horrible question, again and

again. the same as before, but deeper, different now. he sees her walking up the beach, her feet sinking in the sand. he sees her floating across the cafe, casual yet busy. in her foreign way, up and away from the scene, the mess. what are we doing here here? he wonders. where is my place?

its crowded at high tide. the ocean blue is endless, peppered with swimmers and surfers. the line ups are concentrated yet full. the only place to be, he tells himself.

she leaves in the evening. the post midnight escape flight, through Asia, then back to America: her family awaits. the urban ambitions; men and their clean resumes. all dressed in black. already she feels the electric clutter, the street lights. already she shivers at the crowds, the masters of the universe, the shiny cars. there is a price for everything, she thinks to herself. stay with it - never easy, she resolves.

at the beach all the girls are beautiful. never doubt, never deep. sitting in the shade, watching the waves roll in, my thousand pound lover, my liberated invitation, my stoic beliefs.

pretty, he falls in love, again and again. might as well. the life fleeting, he resolves. the time short. the opportunity to be great, again and again. a daily gamble, an exhausting lifetime. and here we are, daily, progression, through it.

you don't know me, Henry tells her.

yes i do, she replies.

all you easy riders better watch your step.....

down at the beach its night again. the boys shuffle around, the girls are still beautiful.

don't know nothing about nothing. the city lights so far away - we are holding fast to this little paradise, this alcove, this Herculean dream. never end....never end..... the angels smile upon us.

they are silicone, and i love them, she triumphantly announces.

she sits straight, back to the mirrored wall. she has been a hustler and a magnet. a mogul and a sinner. i wanna be a monster, she muses. i wanna be a fuck machine.

the moon is out there, somewhere. but now, in the sunshine, sprawled out, magnificent, alive, and when the saints arrive, and when the clouds burn off, its back to promiscuity, back to the machine.

you can fuck her, but you cannot love her, and that is just what you need. so The Gods say.

girl i wanna be your dog.

*

Jamu

oh morning blues, oh easy day - just awash, with the rock and roll beachside hati hat. always on the run, always got the lingo. jazz jazz, groovy groovy, the water whispers. fun times and new acid obituaries. take take - the moment you wake up, from freedom to concentration camp. the bathroom is a great place to fuck - the beach is a wonderful place to fall in love. don't mean a think if it ain't got that swing - now here we go.

the trenches, the shapes, the single fins, the heart break; character and fat rails, everyone eats for free. good morning Christmas Day, hello MCA. preach me a love song, sing me that lovely gangster melody. the finest place in Bangkok, the easiest girls on the Bukit. don't need no more friends, ain't got a dime to my name. on the freeway doing 30, down the stairs, nice and slow.

maybe we get a birthday cake this year, maybe we smile some more. my passion and your eyes - anywhere you want to go. a soft melody and a stack of dollars - loose the pretense, keep the sand. all your shiny shoes don't mean a thing in the jungle. calm and mellow, with some moonshine, wild, growling, when the sun goes down. all chi chi pussy pussy under the bright burning sun.

take me back to New York City, Henry muses. what does Harlem look like now?

the groovy rich girls, the urban stares, and courageous smiles.

Lightning Bolts and Disco Girls

on the beach its all Bintang and booty. The Gods sparkle angel dust on all the elevated connoisseurs. magic on a monday, cant chase her anymore. ain't thought about real love, in quite some time. a bit of jamu, a slice of paradise, another beautiful butterfly, an infinite snapshot. here are the keys, The Gods say. spend the whole night with her.

mama and her downtown sugar shack, Jimi Hendrix and his wonderfully wild hair. open the door delirium, bring me a beautiful french girl who makes me shiver. all the antiquated fashions, all the macho poetry for the evening sessions. hey you! hey lovely! a little bit of kiss kiss, a modern romance to pass the time. still 3 feet high, always fun.

watch her go in and out. send her a ray of sunshine and a new Gucci hat. all about how much you give.... Marilyn Monroe and another spiritual selfie. beautiful, never really left. a blank stare, a smile and a lot of heart; new funk beach living, raw, with dirty love on the side.

a little to the left, The Gods say. everything is gonna be alright now.

*

Nature And Women

what a pity. what a short beach romance. what do the heroes have to say?

tempestuous, growling, fully awake; theory and cataclysms at 11:30am. meet me for a taste, join the band after sunset. high up, special, raging – just let The Gods do their thing. a bit less cash, a few more waves. down and out, back on the beat – sama sama.

blue and beautiful, sacred because she says so. easy betty – gotta go darling. a crack at the tittle, a cool place to hang under the pesky moonshine. nature and girls, soothes the savage beast. hati hati – its all love now.

never know what the winds might do – she comes when she

BEAUTIFUL DECISIONS, HEROIC CHOICES

is ready – all you need to know. the sacred dance, the fast lane to enlightenment. always with the sun, always out the back. the girls sit around and watch, the boys play hard with the sharks. the bedroom and that damn fan, the cafe and those bathing beauties. everywhere we go – all the time, because Larry Levan said so.

breaks deeper, smiles a lot.

it ain't the fortune, it ain't the casket. best to say it like it is; under the wood ship and dreaming, my favorite drum and bass catalogue, my treasonous homies whom just don't get it. the tide is coming back up, the boys act cool; the girls chat up their computer screens. you gorgeous mess, you partially blooming hippy – space ball madness, a stack of fifties because you care. what happened to the super bowl? where did the honesty go?

super cosmic – many road I've known...... just eating up the time, just lost in those eyes. a model citizen – she is hanging with the girls tonight, but she really doesn't know why. an artist and a fantasy ocean dream – she watches the boys stride up and down the beach, just because they told her to. what would Neil Cassidy do? whats the story with them pills? is the work really that important? are we truly tragically alone? the morning musings, the soft touch of water......

the evening, she whispers the eternal questions, badgered by beauty and testament. your eyes they glow; your smile is infectious. a mature relationship; a wonderful heart is all you need. her young crooked smile and sarcastic monotone voice, makes the beast breath easy, and the masters do their thing. a long delirious spell of hati hat – my grand coochie sweetheart, the ariel specialists, the concentrated DJ celebrities, the laughter that everyone in the sand longs for.

clean water, she looks at her watch again, and pushes past the boulders, up the hill, again and again. master of war, dying for peace (ahimsa, he reads across all the groovy stone walls); we've come all this way simply because of a beat longing and an all night date with The Gods. so groovy, so special! love is a frantic genius, a complete unified theory. we are here – this is now.

happening - my dainty kook sit in, my long way from home dialogue. mazultuff and Molotov cocktails - damn fine to see you again Burt Russel! welcome to the funhouse.

Nothing says love like seating placements. nothing says motherfucker like a short wave and a grin. Iggy Pop is upstairs, Elvis is down on the beach. Daddy says its about the money, but no one really knows.

the mix tapes keep you limber, the mess hall is a whore house. take a number, get in line.

Adrock just walked in. Its clean and head high out at the point. club paradise, here we come. good evening Mona Lisa, welcome home Jackson Pollack. you may have to die a little more, you might just bleed out right here, in the sand, under the stars, alone and hungry. promised nothing, in search of cosmic meditations all day and all night. better believe - better when she is happy. love is a good bass line, home is where the music is clear. simple white girls and fearless beasts - my brother, my Brutus, my Jesus killer.

star? perhaps. but that don't really matter now. all for a few shots at immortality; all for my mama and her poet dream.

the cool girls get into it. the Universe takes care of you always. nature, women, and a bit of cool music - thanks Universe, he hears you Jimi.

Brussel Sprout settles in for the full emotional space walk. perfect pitch, lovely garden. we are growing surfboards and vegetables, welcome aboard!

of course she is a vegetarian.

the more you care, the more it hurts. the girls eat down on the beach, in the low slung plastic chairs, from the pricey fish menu. Brutus tries to slide in through the back door - its a wonderful mess, its a long story for the boom boom kids and the hipster rose beds, always blooming. if it were your first time then you might not believe it were all so real. but thats the gift - but thats the junk pile. a slow walk back to Duval Street, a cool shuffle down Central Park West.

i got a plan, she says.
cool cool, Henry solemnly replies.
how was it out there? she asks.
clean and beautiful, he dutifully replies.
a great alchemist, stuck on a very busy island. the sound of water, the smell of sand; treacherous - you brute, you wild magnet, you poor heart throb - its always wonderful, its always honest.
dinner with the girls, she tells him.
have a great time, he says with a smile. gone to the slaughterhouse, back up on the mountain.
it ain't easy, Shiva says. but it sure is fun.

*

Poetry Beach Girl Days

beach beach, wild wild; from one to another, The Gods they are amused, the masses they cower.
another year, another promise - imagine this is how it is, forever, with the frangipani flowers and the taste of pussy; with the sugar and honey and mango; with the pale southern girls and the smart young angels. imagine the music never stops playing, the sky is always clear. the butterflies lie in the sun, every square inch of destitution for a five fingered slap of fame. they took out the jungle, they inserted the white women. relentless circumstance and useless power - a new naughty love affair - some time alone to marinate. no whining, no worries. easy does it; this one may hurt.
you could of had us both, she says coyly. clear across the bathroom floor, armed with a sledgehammer, what a pity, such a fool you are.
tell me something dirty, he says.
something dirty? she wonders. like mud, she replies sarcastically.
you regret not being with her? Garbanzo asks.

yes, Henry replies.
dirty girl, Garbanzo says.
my weakness, Henry admits.
all this quizzical time and thats all it took, Garbanzo realizes.
simple as that, Henry answers.

the tides are low, the equation is simple. she looks at him and gets wet. instantly. she hangs around waiting for someone to fuck her. she never asks, she never says no. she reads the heavy fashion periodicals from back home, she puts his toes in her mouth, looks up at him with those lunatic eyes and promises to make it all better.

yeah, but do they know how to love? Garbanzo asks.
who knows, Larry Levan says.
who cares, Brussel Sprout lazily sighs.
girls with short pants are always welcome, Einstein hammers. now everybody get the fuck out so i can work!

the architect gets her shimmy on; the city girls spell trouble and desperately hope they don't catch anything.
just making something beautiful, Henry thinks.
just watching the waves, the boys say.

kisses, thunder, love and a handful of sand; never ending, hot as hell. my enduring fantasy, my beautiful rock and roll. it is what you want it to be – sama sama. married a music man....just cause.....daddy has no idea, the pastors are appalled. certainly a competition, certainly a hang with the real beach side hommies. getting down with the first class harpoon squad, a fine time to go down on her. a lovely day for poetry-stay just like that and someone will notice. you want some? you get it now?

its a silent revolution, just sit here and watch the fools run by. ain't got nothing to hide, ain't got nothing to hold. so precious, alluring, the wind and the possibility; Garbanzo does up the snaps on his red velvet shirt and walks back up the hill with dignity and authority.

is it ok? he asks.

better be, Einstein tells them. now look at this bitchin paint job.

brutal: the sunshine, the girls.

so heavy, Garbanzo comments.

painful, the butterflies lay out and imagine that nothing matters. possession, booty, money, touch; my easy girl, my second lover and her tempting spells. softer, gentle, obscene; no hate, all love.

champagne preachy, believe: the curls, the vegetables – annihilated, momentous, healthy. groovy love tool, honey wars and your savage cool. a daily miracle; just a taste, again hati hati. tied up for hours while the funny Asian inspects the pretty knots.

when are we going to fuck? Jezebel asks.

just be cool, The Gods say.

it ain't with the kids, it ain't on the rock – we practice, yes; a tribe without the wars. beautiful again, masters and their thin skins. a long heroic walk out, a sledgehammer to prove it legitimate. just before sunset and the beats kick in, and the longboard girl gets the short little right hand screamer to make all the Bra Boys cheer.

Henry still has the wack job cheer leader from the Bronx on tap.

just what we do, Einstein says to the American holiday school teacher. he slides in close; don't ask no questions, ain't got no doubts.

love or big checks – which one you want? Einstein asks politely. cause i only got the pockets for one, he finally concludes.

the sun may never go down, the hour may never turn.

★ Part *two*

LIGHTNING BOLTS
AND
DISCO GIRLS

*

Sama sama, she says, and strips off her pants.

Mercy, the catwalk, the silver screen, written in gold, hovering about, the absolute 9th street burn magnet;
A bottle of champagne, a cool case of scurvy, written in red, up all night with the Russian, greedy down in Seminyak;
An offshore moment, planted organic and grown local, pretending to be fabulous, just hanging in the cafes when the sun is out;
Another open relationship, another barrel......
Punchy, made to order, with tinted hair and a Tennessee smile - over and over again, hemorrhaging when she says hello - that's what the juice man said.

Mercy, down by the shore, kicking up sand, low down and pretty, walking around with nothing to do, always from somewhere else;
The first drop of poison, the wild eyes and setting sun - again for the DJ, again for the boys;
Mixer and Molotov cocktail time, spinning out of control, oblivious - once and always lost, professional, in turmoil and peace;

Burning, for that small curve in the hip, that wind and waste –
  mantras and maps, keeps that cool......all day long;
Definitive, the best time ever, this lifetime, watching all the
  sand blow away;
Please make us something special, please order yourself a gun
  – bigger days and daisy smiles, take your pants off again, give
  us all a look.

Music here – dreamy and sexy.......

Maybe it's make believe, maybe it's a promise – whatever you
  decide it is, however you want to lay down, pushy and bright,
  worn out, just above the knees;
Play me a song, deal me a heartbreak – the Russian girls and
  moonlight hippies, for the wanton prep school pedigree and
  the German stripper girls;
No need to apply, no one to write home about – X marks
  that pirate smile and wandering fool habit – paid well for
  being pretty;
Sama sama, she says, and undoes another button.

*Busted flat in Baton Rouge, waiting for a train, was feeling nearly
faded as my jeans / Bobby thumbed a diesel down, just before it
rained / rode it all the way to New Orleans.*

Up and down the court, back and forth across the beach,
  around the cliff and parched for a little drop of poison;
Flashbulb parades, and wild off color remarks for the police
  chief, the rum runner, the juice angel – another carrot please,
  another monster truck driver;
Charisma, silver, full time – the headlines are a thousand miles
  away, the big names don't hold all the same weight in this
  hemisphere;
Everyday you resound to leave, everyday you write something
  new;

LIGHTNING BOLTS AND DISCO GIRLS

Another paragraph, another sweetheart.....
Satvic music with a lot of style, dressed in black, drowning in
   the Peninsula, never going home – they just want to eat you
   there.

More style please, more gado gado – with a whimpering
   smile and a short term promise, permanently dazed by all
   the scantily clad Brazilian girls;
Stuck on.......what the fuck are they all stuck on?

Fuck, she said;
Now, I said;
What are you to me? she asked;
An enigma, I said;
Why an enigma? she asked;
Because you don't know what the fuck I am.

(Music here, dreamy, sexy and smooth)

Pushing, the heightened pulse, those suicide titties;
First time around The Apple, lost and mobile, strung out on
   23, and trying – the medicine, the party girl blues;
Imagine this very moment, now imagine it without me......the
   voice, just the voice; a touch up, just a little touch up.....
All the talented, all the destitute, playing Kind Of Blue for the
   offshore Attica groupies; once around the park, just to show
   my baby the lights;
Drive me down 5th Avenue, pick me up on Labuan Sait;
don't mean a thing, fuck fuck fuck, don't mean a thing......;
You're fun, she said;
Yeah, put your hand right here.......

Uptown it's brownstones and napalm, on the coast it's bend
   over and shuck the fuck up.
Just making friends, just blowing up;

Lightning Bolts and Disco Girls

A little slower, a mellow dip to the left – lean back, turn it up a
    bit, magnanimous and cumming – now we are really
    friends, now we really fucked it up;
Back on the streets they get a buck a page for this; better not
    try anything else, this part of the film is special.......
Make me a slow burn, take out another Picasso; no bullshit, no
    talking; the more honest you are, *the more they want to
    fuck you;*
Now break – don't worry about nothing;
Keeping it underground, that's the hard part.

Watch me move, all up and down, I'm a tea tree, I'm a balloon;
Elephant dreams, master at the beach break blues and yogi
    well wishes – permanently at the track, long shot and heavy
    bru – been out all night, been wet all day – check out all this
    foam, dusty and beautiful, aging with grace, even with the
    dirt and the sweat and the shinny white girls who won't
    give it up;
A sparkling night sky, a longboard romance and an ounce of
    ginger – just what mama thinks I'm doing, just what the
    sand told me to be – allegories and pleasantries, the older
    gals small talk at the counter and bounce back to the
    spinning wheel, while I get all groovy to this two step, and
    slide up on this stranger:
(nah, really girl, where you from?)

You so special, you so hot; pretty pretty, so I'm a take two.......
Call up Gerry, get Miki on the line, fuck them hard stares and
    heart ache specialists;
this shit got out of hand, this message went left.

Mr. Heavy steps into the limelight:
I was just in the bedroom fucking this girl while her friend sat
    in a chair next to the bed and read a book;
What book was it? Henry asks;

LIGHTNING BOLTS AND DISCO GIRLS

Im not really sure, Mr. Heavy replies.

The creator has a master plan, peace and happiness for every man.

Yeah she's rad, yeah she's pretty, yeah she's all grace and ink –
just another sunny day, hoping that the winds stay offshore;
Yeah, she jumps, from one country to the next: a Himilayan
trail, a Monkey Wrench Gang.....a fit, a new plan, a new coat
of paint, a straight line and a glass full of ginger – save me
Holden, open the gates JD........ groovy baselines and
morning meditations, just like she promised;
A new smile, an elegant trace of blue, bringing it all back – city
child, mamas boy, patron saint, believer, kick flip genius, out
all weekend machine, plagued by the beauty, allowed to
hang with the legends, the big dynamite sea life chronies
– all black and white, grainy, dark, with a purpose, pulling in
deep, housed in gold, wreaking of mercy;
Punchy, flat tailed and wondering – just relax, just be cool –
the red juice and light jazz tunes turns all the whores into
angels......
Admit it, humble and dreaming, with a quick swell and a
tough guy facade, to greet the new wave butterflies with, to
be a saint for......
When Mr. Heavy stays home all night, when the kids spin
for a new Disco crowd, when the ink girls play it cool, but
want to get fucked just like everyone else – that's what the
newspapers mean by weird;
Satu Lagi, he says; mantaap sekali – now pay them bills, drown
in her eyes, orgasm like a star

Be cool boy, just be cool.....

Lightning Bolts and Disco Girls

VALETINO AHIMSA

*

flying, the grand beauty; got a long ride and a cheap tweed suit
 - bargain and beauty, when the sun comes up.
the soft rock and roll chimes through the early haze - the tricks,
 the bikes, the narrow roads and deadly hesitations. another
 name, another night.
(the light is dry, the memories are many).
peaceful - Valentino Ahimsa, with the top down and the beaches
 clean. she lays out, took off those tight jeans, and that cheap
 bra.
you're a creep, she remarks to Valentino.
keep smiling, he says.
mama, you bring the cheap wine and the Italians will bring the
 drums.
its a guaranteed barn burner, and a fancy time with the polished
 mini gurus up on the hill - just like she promised, just like The
 Gods said it would be.
ain't no thing, Soups says. the blues always get front row when
 the fires start.

she shamelessly worries about his situation, while he stirs the
 brew down by the river and hums a little Robert Johnson for
 the passing butterflies.

Lightning Bolts and Disco Girls

ain't so luxurious no more, he tells the withering angels. better
   get back to the beach, where the earth can speak to you
   directly.
smooth wide turns...... Einstein is tagging up the 4 train again.

the anxiety is palpable, in the wealth and the style. hold out
   a daisy and paddle up to the reef – smiling as the cool kids
   hang in the dirty, on the corners, and scribble that Moby
   Dick poetry into the messy journals and shanty town brick
   wall beauties;
paid a fancy sum for the guru and her healing touch – just
   lucky to be here – remember her smile and every touch she
   offers – the Italian boys with the new clean white t shirts
   and the morning smile, to exorcise the party blues and the
   satya style business deals;
mama brought a tattooed angel, better get into the soil while
   its still there.

Valentino Ahimsa – spread the love, in all the lunch boxes, in
   all the bougie bougie sat sung prayer meetings.
a certain perfect oneness, a mystery behind the blue sky.
play the blues, 4 bars, while we wait for Sonny Rollins and
   Lightning Sam Phillips to get the car packed.
a smooth pack of new crisp 50 dollar bills in the back pocket,
   from here to Minnesota, straight through the night.
the Russian girls will all meet us there, just bring the clean
   sheets and the pricey evening tobacco.
clear and easy, the wind blows stronger this morning;
love love – see what happens with the sand castles later on.

the road ways are busy with sun seekers and teenage breakfast
   Bintang delinquents. at every intersection its a noise, a circus,
   a fantasy.
choices are prevalent – everyday you wanna go.

VALENTINO AHIMSA

no money, no honey, Einstein preaches.
casual, even with the light.
a lovely proletariat in paradise, learning, one native word at a time.
the bells, the whispers, about prosperity and also peace; about abundance and sacrifice. in every raindrop a bit of poison, a surprise, for the bards and the expatriated hair dressers. the boss sits at the first table and smokes heavy rolled cigarettes while he studies the weekly numbers: more eggplant, less beat root. all she needs to remember.

five deep at the shala. like this everyday now, she sadly says.
sometimes its almost to much.
but the money comes rolling in. got yourself a hot commodity. got a handful of pennies and no where to go.

Valentino Ahimsa and E=MC squared puts the electric boogaloo rift right back into the punk punk fuck fuck water water tribe.
the magnets have turned around, the Italians have arrived – stick with your own! the Nazis preach. drop in when ever you want.....
pretty cool, black mambo and a shot of jamu – so mellow at the sand side corner office; so much better when the rock and roll comes on.
we are all waiting for Neil Young and the third Raylette to go on. thats Floyd Patterson down there on payphone, talking with Jesus.
stretch it out and be free – Clapton in reds and pinks, Dylan as the preacher; the dusty roads have their penitentiary blues as well, but that wild first lady spends all her coin on moonshine and advertising, so now we sit around and wait for the tides to change, even with the rent due and the payments so near.
just like Gerry said it would be, just like mama promised.

Lightning Bolts and Disco Girls

all around town for a good taste of jamu, all the way down the
beach to say hello; somewhere between passion, love, and
cock sucking, thats where you can find us, every time.
satu lagi, keep it beautiful; never gets dull, never gets heavy.
the saints and their Brooklyn Bridge foreclosures, the pole
dancers and their timeless charms;
going to roll down to B town and score a shiksa and a side of
envy; with her bank account and this thin sarong to cover
up all the good karma with.

the shade is faithful, the sun got her hot dress on.

the kids go banging, the swamis decided to hang in the lazy
afternoon, and preach the Woodstock rumors and Union
Square legends to the jumpy local boys who keep their
fingers on the trigger.

in the back seat Bessie Smith got her side arm and a young sun
soaked blonde boy. could be on the road for awhile - could
be mystical and dreaming, just waiting for her to show up.
the boys are going to bronze Eric Clapton at around 5pm -
you should stick around.
another re telling of Minnie the Moocher, another beach day.
the password is cool, the girls look amazing. just like the wind
grinding, with the professionals sharpening the axe, ready
for her tribulations and stringy legs; dear Mercedes Benz,
dear Lord, the girls ain't got no more lies for the pirates, the
soothing aqua transcendence, even though they deserve the
hammer, the full village green.
twelve cop cars and an empty bottle of influence; stomp on
that distortion pedal and pretend that she still loves you.
it ain't Santa Cruz, it ain't Mysore.
saw a couple of nice ones, he says.
now you are finally listening, The Gods reply.

VALENTINO AHIMSA

somewhere in that guitar solo, watching that nameless hero glide across the face, inching closer to sunset, in love for the first time, hanging in the shade with the electric guitars loud and the cotton fields warm.
no problems, officer. we were just watching the mockingbird, counting the silver coins, wondering why we ain't out there......
a drop of healthy heartbreak, an evening skinny and a cool breeze for the gold smiles and the easy play things.
Valentino Ahimsa! now say my motherfucking name!

my beach poetry and your baby shuffle ought to make The Gods happy.
just like the first time, Axel says. just me and Neil Young on a long train ride for the coast.
never knew it was going to be so dramatic, as it goes.

Django Reinhardt and her hot pink hot shorts, makes the crossroads look a bit more enticing.
the tempests have gone mellow and the frangipani sweethearts are restless; pull up the bridge and drop the bass; breath easy, the Velvets have finally arrived.
gentle young ginger, pure as the new disco warrior boys, calm as the reef; honest flower riddles and the long guitar solos makes me hard.
lazy white boys give the stare down and the crazy guru boys wonder what she looks like without pants on.
then Dixie Moonshine walks in and orders a Hobo without the bread.

may look like Robert Ford, but feel like Jesse James.

turn up the rock and roll, Valentino tells the staff. Dixie might show us a bit of poetry and a shot of skin.
a beautiful woman, but Valentino can't tell her immediately.

Lightning Bolts and Disco Girls

more Dylan! the Butterflies chant.
more rock and roll, Dixie Moonshine writes on the bathroom wall at François's.
the new Maxs Kansas City, the sun soaked Bungalow 8.
hard boys and shanty hippy girls; play it slow and sad, just like Dixie asked for.
Valentino smiles at the setting sun.
so beautiful, so peaceful. as the air cools and the young girls ramble into the Warungs looking for diamonds and salvation. a luscious harp and a frightened darling - Dixie turns the volume back up and makes sure the pirates have their glasses full and their hands busy.
practically a legend, Valentino watches her walk by, and chants a little Om Shanti Shanti to Shiva, and all the good chocolate choir girls.

happy in your Picasso tower? he asks her.
perfectly, she replies.

I was going to be an architect, Dixie tells him. then a diplomat, then a painter, and finally a poet. now i do the door at Paradise Garage and sing in my brothers rhythm and blues band. nothing pays the bills, but nobody cares. came here with nothing, and i'll probably leave here with nothing. i'm fine with that.
she sips her tea and looks out at the dark night and black ocean.
whats your story? she absently asks.
Valentino smiles and leans back in his wood folding chair.
the air is cool tonight, but still humid. there is no place he's supposed to be. nothing he cares to remember right now.
came in just like you, he tells her straight. not yet sure how it all ends up.
she cracks a smile.
as if you care, Valentino says. as if this matters......

VALENTINO AHIMSA

don't be flippant, she tells him. i might just surprise you.
the evening has a hint of anger and defeat. the suffering
   remains in vogue. the fires are just starting. never never – the
   music gets a little louder, the animals begin to stir.

the fresh frangipani and the reformed derelicts, lend integrity
   and a haze of peace. never hoped for something so sweat,
   never been to Mississippi.
the hush, the calm, the community.
strut by, revealed, in love (always), the young Spanish queens
   are moving in, the real estate is going up.
silent, diving, tempting; Valentino watches with a silent smile
   and dreams of her next to him, away from here, where no
   one knows his name and no one says a thing. light,
   memorable, strong – anytime he wants to know. a different
   time, a distant memory. a shallow kiss and a long embrace.
could be anywhere, he thinks. he smiles. resolved.
and we are all slowly dying.
and we are all one.

the dream.....

a taste, just a taste....barely.
greatness. Henry sits and wonders about greatness. someplace
   peaceful and clean, with the fires and the gentility. the
   women and the empty sand beaches.
kindness. Dixie sits and wonders about kindness, from the
   cheap seats at Kisssingers, from the vibrating ends of her thin
   finger tips.
where are we going now? again, the Hobo wonders, and
   Brussel Sprout boards another bus in South America.
could be.....a smile, a wasted opportunity, a wood boat and
   a box of fire crackers. never the home you thought it would
   be..... respect her, she knows you by name and face. she
   dreams for you, longs for you, plays a hit song and drives

the big trucks in for you – for you to handle all the hardness
and fiction; all that standard shine and make believe
ambitions.

nothing to do, investigate the swells – the boys amble around
slow in the morning and predict how big it might get.

she hopes you are alright. your simple beauty – all she longs
for.

Valentino takes her hand and promises to believe.

misty eyes with a searing pulse – dangerous like the moon,
resolved as a king. the vortex is howling, the madness is
contagious. beautiful, long, dark curls, round smiling faces,
suggestive grins. gifts for Athena and Ra, no longer enslaved,
hoping she comes back in time for summer.

push push, the winds are still up, and the Macho Moonshine
calls his sister back home for Sunday services, but she don't
come round no more.

i'm on the head of a needle, she yells back at Macho. ain't had
no sugar in quite some time. but got my eye on a pretty little
pagan. make all my weary dreams come true.

shining, under the bright lights, working like an infected dog.
obviously the darlings have their road maps figured out;
chocolate day dreams and limber freak show artists pay their
somber dues, make their way down to the beach, the sand
whispering dirty love poems and empty blue sky promises.

the cheerleaders are putting their shorts on, getting ready for
the evening session.

hold it Dixie – he still thinks about you.

groovy groovy, love love – while the steel villages burn, we
breath with The Gods. in the simple time, in an age of
wonder and grand rich creations, hands deep in the salt
water, in the sand, under the sun, along the mat, caressing
the skin.

my lovely wild dandelion, my deep morning affairs – learning
with the kings, easy with the angels.
this is your chance to do something special, with your damn
time and your damn life. don't waste it on wind and cheap
women; don't squander on anger and indecision. don't
worry about doing what you love. be simple and graceful.
smooth wide turns. all you need to do.

Einstein preaches from the mountain top, then retreats back
into his shaping room.
Super bueno! Henry admits.
everybody back to my place! Mr Heavy announces.

Valentino watches the angry working girls from a corner seat
and sends the love.
not a word, he tells himself. important not to fuck up with
the small talk.
groovy groovy, love love – Valentino reads a day old Herald
Tribune thats been left in the kitchen. a rare find around
these sandy parts. he is lost in the riots and the beheadings;
the land wars and constant recriminations. he reads the
business dealings and billion dollar advancements. he reads
about the weather machines and the West Africa out breaks.
he follows the liberals and the conservatives, the blacks and
the whites, the hate and the hope. he sees the faces of
familiar leaders and nameless thugs. he fingers the obituaries
and the baseball scores. he feels dizzy and incomplete.
worried and alone.

Valentino Ahimsa walks down to the beach and burns the
newspaper in a small hole. he buries the ashes under the
sand.
he bends his neck back and faces his head to the blue sky and
warm sun.
the warmth settles him again. grounds. he breathes deeply and

Lightning Bolts and Disco Girls

forces a smile, closes his eyes tight, clenches his lips, and gives thanks to The Gods, and is reassured of his exile.
still super cool, still silent in the sun.
you take the fickle beauty, you gave the fading love.
the ghost of Dicky Betts, the growl of Bessie Smith.

Valentino goes back to the corner, and scribbles the morning words, for his first time sweetheart, long gone.

THE ELEPHANT AND THE BAD MOTHERFUCKER

*

1.

The dream is a crystal, she says. Here you go, have a taste.
And she hands him a piece of her heart, and he clumsily chokes on the first bite.

Am learning to be cool, The Elephant tells her. I'm a late bloomer.
Better hurry up, she says.
Am trying the slow route, he says. To revel in the mistakes.
She grunts, turns up the radio, gazes out the front doorway, and wonders what is the price for all this beauty and courage today?
Ever loved an Elephant? he asks her. Ever been here, but, not really? he says.
She leans in, clears her throat, delights in the mischief and confusion, lashes a rusty line to his furious heart, and tugs like a bad motherfucker.

Just don't know, he continues. Just another......just the silence and deadly passion of it all.
You can be anything, she tells him. No matter where we go. No matter what happens – it's all a long night; it's all a special

interest group.

I'm wet and special, she continues. This late night neighbor fly by is just what I wanted.

The Elephant folds his fingers around the sun, puckers his lips, and rips his chest clean open.

Deadly, The Sun whispers.

Only if you continue to think about her, Miss Universe advises. The coveted taste of sorrow and salt....hmm.

Better get a new zoot suit and a one way ticket to Mesopotamia, The Gods chant in unison.

This jungle is going to kill you, because all this part time love is hand cuffed to a Las Vegas bed post, and it just gets worse.

As if you didn't know, Bad Motherfucker tells him. This vodka twist, this endless punk ceremony; this incredible ability to care, all distraught and restless, and still fucked up all the time.

Miss Universe fights back a bit, and bites The Elephant square on the third eye.

Told you not to fuck with that girl, Miss Universe tells The Elephant. Is it truly worth the heartache?

Sure, The Elephant nods, like a simple idiot, again.

Miss Universe shakes her head in disbelief. Bad Motherfucker smiles innocently.

I just don't know what I do, Bad Motherfucker feebly admits.

If it's deep, and true, then the silence will heal, and the time will act as a necessary elixir, Miss Universe tells him. You have no idea now, and that's such a wonderful place to be, she continues. Your tight rope, your mansion – head directly for the heart, for that is where the peace and gold truly lays.

The Elephant hears Jimi Hendrix in the kitchen. He sees Charles Mingus walk in the door. He smells the salt water dripping off of a disgruntled Derek Hynd.

All my great friends! The Elephant triumphantly howls, and

THE ELEPHANT AND THE BAD MOTHERFUCKER

allows the illusion to sooth his restless soul.
It is whatever we say it is, Bad Motherfucker tells him. Her lips pursing and red, her voice foreign and crooked.
It is a night out in Hollywood, a butcher shop on the Lower East Side, she continues. Feel me – I'm much better that way.

A raspy beach, a baptism at dawn, with the local children all smashing the piñata around back.
Your center of the universe is closing, Bad Motherfucker tells him. Im a gift, but temporary, she confides.
It doesn't matter the past, the ferocity and mistrust; you are here now, Miss Universe suggests.
Kiss her hand, make her smile.
We came for the peace, The Elephant tells Miss Universe. We came for the sincerity, the strength, the salt water and the dragons. You pretend to be the rock star, yet you get the tax bills just like everybody else.
Drown in it, taste her memory, Miss Universe tells him straight.
See her frowning face – this way to Harlem, this way to CBGB's.
Drunk on air and sun and dirt; am awake early and valiant, with the cowboys and the captains.
I'm cooking your soul, Bad Motherfucker admits to The Elephant. I'm very good at it, she says lightly.
Nobody visits The Captain. Nobody views the mantra prose and antique poetry.
Still a derelict, Bad Motherfucker observes. Still madly in love.

At the seas lonely edge The Elephant lays on his round stomach and writes love letters to The Sun.
This morning you gave me life, The Elephant writes. This evening you gave me sorrow.
Open your arms, ask nothing, believe nothing; accepting it all, perspiring, singing lovely, tramping along the beach, filthy for another day, The Sun writes back.

Mellow, The Elephant confides. Resilient and able.

Welcome home, Miss Universe tells him. Parading around the jungle, with nothing to do.

You might be pretty, The Jungle tells The Elephant. But that doesn't mean much anymore.

The Elephant wipes the sand from his palms on a peach colored sarong that hangs from the garage door.

This is me naked, The Elephant admits. Now you know what few others know. Love me the most now, though I deserve none of it, he confides.

Listen to my spine, The Elephant continues. Hold my energy, bathe in the molecules that force themselves from out of my body; without that foreign touch, the nights are cold, and the mornings are empty.

(Miss Universe digs at the nearest hole, and crawls inside).

Pass me by, Bad Motherfucker instructs The Elephant.

I don't know how, The Elephant replies.

Don't be sad, she tells him directly, with an arrow and a flame in each eye. It is just starting......

Thunder nods his heavy head, and Lightning closes her silver eyes.

We give you the circle, Miss Universe says. Don't fuck it up.

For my neighbor, who makes me smile, your Bad Motherfucker.
The Elephant scribbles across the fresh morning sky; now forever silent, yet still a ranting fool.

What is in our heart? What is in our actions? What is In our speech? Speak the truth, move forward, be kind.
Miss Universe scribbles her prescription along the edge of The Elephant's new born heart. And he quickly rises from the milky waters, proceeds forward, deeper, and forgets it all.......

THE ELEPHANT AND THE BAD MOTHERFUCKER

All love; be all love, Miss Universe directs him.

The Elephant sinks into a trance, out of the body, deep into the void, and he witnesses himself in a cage, curled up and cold, naked, with a thin white stained sheet wrapped around him, shivering and scared, hiding from the world.

The Elephant sees a small ray of sunlight through a cell window high above the floor, and the figure under the sheet reaches for the light (the warmth and the health), yet falters, tired and worn, the figure retreats back into the recesses of damp shadows and deep chills.

Thats my soul, The Elephant says to Miss Universe. Thats my weakness.

With his shivering strength and growing composure, The Elephant searches for something true within himself; a remedy, an elixir, the fuel for the frightened spirit, huddled in the dull empty corner.

That's my soul, The Elephant tells Miss Universe again. And again The Elephant searches for something deep within himself. He investigates his stomach, his head, his chest, until he arrives at the heart, and there is a slight burst of hope, a flash and a song.

We are here, The Elephant hears. We are one.

The Elephant delves into the heart, fully immersed, and arrives suddenly at a spring of endless clean cool water, where he kneels, and sips, and feels the elixir over his mouth, down his scratchy throat, into his barreling chest, until finally the juices drown out the poisonous flames of a mad rage, and the soul's perilous cage is gently flooded with strength and hope.

Free now! The Elephant is slowly nourished back to life. Slowly standing, alone, moving forward, shining and surprisingly straight, mesmerized forever by the allusive attraction of the fearless sun and loyal sky.

Miss Universe bows her beautiful head, and her long locks of fire red hair falls in front of her clear face.

Exhausted, The Elephant admits.

Alive, Miss Universe tells him.

All dressed in orange, passing the time, with vendors and various searchers, The Jungle puts an ounce of salt between her thighs, and a sash of gold over her bold shoulders.

Take this to the sea, The Jungle says to the Bad Motherfucker.

We need you to care for us, we need you to love him.

At what price? Bad Motherfucker asks. I have my cabin in the thickets. I have my sour but resilient roots; my throbbing dance and ridiculous work. How am I to care for a fallen angel and his burning skyscrapers? Why am I to be the only pearl in a yearning sea?

Because you are the pearl! The Jungle demands.

Don't worry, its all been written, its all been painted, The Jungle continues.

His hands are sweaty and nothing makes sense, but we know, this green leaf and I; we know, and that is all which matters now.

The Jungle opens her hand and passes the Bad Motherfucker a vial of cold spring water and a stone. The Jungle smiles wide, blows her a kiss, then lays down in the dark burnt dirt, and hums a Louis Armstrong tune, while the pale moon hangs low in the sleeping sky.

2.

A continuing sign of proof that I know nothing, The Elephant confesses.

Miss Universe frowns, shakes her kind head in disbelief, and touches The Elephant at his third eye, relieving him of all pain, all desire, and all the vicious wanting.

Tonight was a simple test, Miss Universe tells The Elephant softly. And you passed. You listen, you let go of desire, you let go of the past; you build your strength, your vision, your dream; then suddenly you are solid, like a diesel freight engine, and nothing but purpose affects you.

Miss Universe picks a small black cherry from Saturn's third ring, and hands it to The Elephant.

Wearily, Elephant takes the cherry, cool and moist, from out of her hand, and he touches her palm slightly, and is momentarily light again, sliding down a slippery rainbow, fast and out of control, speeding across the dark star speckled cosmos, floating, with the galaxy endless on either side of him.

A choir of angels look down upon him – a soulful Ray Charles, a strong Jackie Robinson, and a wise Nelson Mandela – and they nod their heads in unison, smiling on The Elephant, making sure he does not fall from the path, even as The Elephant tries so hard to fuck it up for himself.

Damn fool, Ray Charles says flatly.

Silly white Elephant, Nelson Mandela says, with a humorous guff.

He has no idea that everything is going to be alright.

Worries like a teenage girl, Jackie Robinson jokes.

Nelson cups his hands together and yells at The Elephant. 'I got you son......!'

The Elephant goes speeding by, from one void to the next. Then suddenly it all stops, and The Elephant returns to his heavy thick skinned body with a silent thud.

Better when it's a little hard, Miss Universe tells The Elephant sternly. Just enough to know you care.

There is a pause.

The Elephant pulls up a chair, sits down between Heartbreak and Freedom, and orders a dragon bowl, no seaweed, a large ginger tea, and a coconut cookie.

We haven't seen you around here for awhile, Heartbreak says.

I've seen him out by the beach quite a bit, Freedom comments.

Lightning Bolts and Disco Girls

- Huh, Heartbreak says. Guess you finally found a sharp razor blade to pass the time with.
- The Elephant drops his head, exhausted, and manages a thin smile, for his two new best friends.
- That says it all, Freedom remarks. A handful of cash and a beautiful Star to test your theories on. If you rolled down to the city with those fantasies, surely you'd be dead or rich by now.
- Watch out for the A train, Heartbreak cautions. Takes a young man to The Love Machine, without fail, every time.
- One way ticket, Freedom says grandly, with a wide cheerful smile.
- And nobody comes back from her.
- The Elephant lifts his hand to his forehead.
- This is the gun, he says lightly. All the colors, so bright, so messy.
- When Peter Fonda sat in that chair he was drowning in ecstasy and tripping like a madman, Freedom tells The Elephant.
- He swore that we were all dead. That this was a dream. He flashed that million dollar rebel smile at Heartbreak over there, and tried to bed down that Raw Angel at the door, who takes all the tickets.
- Said he had a place for her, up in the hills, with a stunning view of the city. Said he was just a shell of a man, with no where to sleep, no one to love, and no where to be. He had fire in his eyes, and misery in his voice. He claimed to own the chains and the water. Said there was no where else to be but right here. Then he went out honky tonking with Charley Mingus one night, and we never saw him again.
- Mix together all that blood and water, Heartbreak laughs, and it's bound to produce a hit one of these days.
- At least its over, Freedom says.
- Never know, Heartbreak replies.

Just playboys playing in the sand, Bad Motherfucker tells The

THE ELEPHANT AND THE BAD MOTHERFUCKER

Jungle. Foolish heart throbs and ambitious bums.
The Jungle smiles in agreement.
They all want to climb on my shoulders, Bad Motherfucker says.
Everybody wants to be here. Everybody wants to be free.
It's love versus motherfucker, The Jungle laments.
Only *you* can tell which, Miss Universe confides.
Sometimes there feels like no difference, Bad Motherfucker says. Sometimes I don't know.
That's not *completely* true, Miss Universe says with a knowing smile.
You know, she tells Bad Motherfucker. You just don't want to admit it.

On the beach, by the sharp rocks, a small pool of lichen gathers, under the shanty moon, where they proceed to pair up in twos, and dance the night away.

Takes a lot of courage, Bad Motherfucker finally says.
The most, Miss Universe confides.
A long night sets in, again; an open heart surgery, a quest for realization; a slow tune to romance the soul with, a missed connection........
Taken, bereaved, done.
Bad Motherfucker undresses under the weeping moonlight, and easily wades into the water. She dances with the urchin and the sharks, the currents and the salt. A thousand dead sailors rise up at the oceans weary edge, and promise her candy, roses, and song.
They watch her smile at the gambling stars, and wrestle the traveling souls. She has no ambivalence – is not injured or lost. She simply flows, from one damaged affair to the next, wrapped in the silver tinsel of love and adventure every time; another loathsome poet, another bleeding dandy.
The strength comes from within, she whispers to The Gods.

You taught me that.

And when she exits the water, and strides handsomely up the beach, The Stars fold their cards, and The Gods are speechless.

The Elephant sits alone at the beach, under a lovely palm tree, listening to the wind at sunset. He sinks into the sand, feels the grains against his lower back, and is warmed by the last bit of sun light.

The Elephant is transfixed on the ocean before him – the waves, the white foam, the deep blue mystery, the brutal indifference.

Nobody knows, The Elephant thinks to himself. And still we keep moving forward.

Peace and love, all peace and love, The Elephant suddenly says.

Miss Universe shoots a sharp glance at The Jungle, and they both smile, deeply bonded, finally calm, assured, without the cluttered nuances.

They simultaneously look towards The Elephant, and they see a new man, like a child preparing to leave home for the first time, and they let the wind surround him, and the water cover him, and the sunlight warm him; they let the empty cosmos believe in him, and the dainty stars to care for him.

Young warrior, Miss Universe pronounces, you've found a unique swell in the circuitous cavern of that raging heart you bury within your thick chest. Enter, roam, delight – the light you see is eternal; it is a simple definition of forever, and you shall view the succeeding whims and stumbles with the full radiance of imagination, desire, and service.

There is no here or there; there is no yesterday, nor tomorrow.

Simply the perfunctory being of now. And your simple words, your plain texts, your raw abstractions, are the compass with which your vessel of years and seconds shall continuously navigate.

Fear not young Elephant, everything has already been written;

everything has been decided; you travel now with a lighter
pack, and charmed directions, along this wild circuit of time
and yearning.
Only you are handsome, only you are great; fear not the jellies
of Rome, or the stabbings of London; under your feet is
dirt and water, all you need to meditate upon, all you need
to know.
We sing to you daily, they recite. Simply listen, and grow
strong.
Peace and love, The Elephant slowly whispers again, and sobs,
for the remainder of his blissful days.

3.

Bad Motherfucker hops a one way Greyhound Bus for the
coast.
She carries a potted rubber plant in one hand, and a small
varnished wooden harp in the other. Her hair falls neatly
past her shoulders, and there is a secret in her lively eyes.
She smiles at the daily routines behind her, and winks at the
despair. She strides along with a small sack of sand and dirt
hanging lazily from her shoulders. She floats by the hustling
telephone lines and whistling cash registers, with a fresh
wound across her chest, and a sweat taste upon her lips.
This is oblivion, she thinks to herself. This is the crossroads.
I've one last door to enter, one last party to attend.

She stands under a flashing red neon light that reads 'SAVIOR,'
and instructs the graying clouds to be kind.
The ground is hard and the air is cool, when the Beat Poets
and Black Panther runaways go strolling by, in orange jump
suits, humming a Curtis Mayfield ballad, telling everyone
that Iggy is dead.
She watches in piercing delight, fueled by destruction and
hope, and gently reminds herself to love more.

Lightning Bolts and Disco Girls

There is no right way, she tells herself. There is no perfect.
She watches her delicate features being etched onto the side of a large granite cliff opposite the station, and she adjusts her smile accordingly, hoping that there is enough pocket money to make her look *more* accurate.
Nothing but money and time, she jokes to herself. My only two friends left. And she switches the weight, from one shoulder to the other.

This is your first time? a man standing next to her kindly asks.
Always feels that way, she says, without turning her head.
He agrees with a heavy sigh. He shuffles his feet slightly, and stands a bit closer to her.
This is always the route I take, the man tells her.
Must be comfortable, she says.
Not particularly, he replies. But I always get there.
She turns her head and looks the stranger up and down: a long, tan, well tailored trench coat, free of wrinkles. A shiny pair of black Prada loafers. No facial hair. A black bowlers hat with a flat red rose leaf neatly tucked into the brim, pulled low over his smiling face.
He looks healthy, sincere, resilient. His eyes are a straight brown, and they chant experience and devotion. His hands are firm, clean and empty. She sees no baggage next to him. She sees no company.

My name is Bad Motherfucker, she tells him gently.
Hello, he dutifully replies. My name is Greatness.
He extends his arm towards her, and she shakes his hand, and smiles surprisingly, honest and free. They remain with hands locked for some time, examining the others face, attempting to read each others current thoughts.

It is the best party ever, Greatness says with an easy grin.
It is *now*, Bad Motherfucker replies smartly.

THE ELEPHANT AND THE BAD MOTHERFUCKER

They step back from each other, turn towards the mountains, and watch The Sun again retreat behind the jagged peaks and brave ridge lines. The sky is suddenly a glow with creams, yellows and reds. A spray of purple and green, a moment of success and welcomed melodrama.

They share a long simultaneous exhalation, the wandering fools, Bad Motherfucker and Greatness, as they board the bus together.

They climb up the short steep stairwell and into the narrow empty aisle, clean yet sticky under their feet.

They listen to the befuddled ancient poetry that the driver automatically recites, as they file towards the back of the coach, easily locate two empty seat next to each other, and settle in, for the long curvaceous ride back home.

EPILOGUE

I'm a motherfucker, The Elephant says, flatly. All I want to do is love and sleep.

You had your chance, Miss Universe tells him harshly.

You are beautiful, The Elephant tells her quickly.

He tries his charms in vain, The Jungle shrugs.

The stars are watching you, Miss Universe tells The Elephant.

And what about her? The Elephant asks sheepishly.

Miss Universe shoots a quizzical gaze at The Jungle, and The Jungle nods her head in affirmation.

Miss Universe looks to the stars, and their infinite youth, and their melancholy atrophy, and she tilts her head to one side, closes her magenta colored eyes, breathes deeply, and kills The Elephant again.

Everyday you dream of color, then cover yourself in mud, Miss Universe tells The Elephant.

Just leave it alone. Just be an angel.

The Elephant sits in a queer silence, watches his last sunset, and ponders the pebbles peppered along the black sand. He follows a seagull effortlessly gliding across the dulling horizon. He listens to the waves arrive with joy against the sharp cliff faces below.

This is again forever, The Elephant thinks to himself. This is the final sonnet, the end to an nfinite poem, the flame slowly extinguishing.

He turns to Miss Universe and feebly attempts a smile.

And still I don't know, he says to her dryly, with fear and anticipation. And still I don't know.....

Miss Universe reaches out her hand, and with a thin golden finger, gently touches his third eye, completely, then let's him go.

Goodbye Elephant, she calmly whispers. Hello love.

THE ELEPHANT AND THE BAD MOTHERFUCKER

Lightning Bolts and Disco Girls

LOS ANGELES

*

1.

the spree and headaches;
the machine guns and the satisfaction of less ordinary, on all
   the t shirts.

the Florida girls just pulled up, the sun just came out;
Perceptions and mid level felonies – amassing stock in all the
   hot young intellectuals;
if you can be ensconced in peace....... the avenues beating
   with fresh rock and roll chimes (you never know).
hustlers, daily dealers, the girls are cheap, amassing fortunes
   on Pacific Avenue;
all in, all groovy – the beat box and the fantasy samples, in
   wild grafitti, alone.

my baby put those high heals on and went to work.....

bless the child and his satvic sideways esteem – its twenty
   dollars out, and another twenty to the beach;
dancing, the dream survives, simple and empty, hotel room
   silence, monsters of agriculture and science, alive at noon;

money, hot sauce, elevated, they cue up for the good looking
   girls, for a taste of infinity, at a bus stop on Vine.
the Mexican girls shimmy, the white hustlers count – damn
   this room is clean!
happy with just this scat.

2.

her blue eyes, her long time promise, all the dudes ask her
   out, all the stars are busy looking beautiful – just what you
   need;
endless – as she leans over the pool table and stares;

(they want you to purchase more).

the radio is another rich girl, penetrating, tight black pants,
   dirty pink sneakers, a gold wrist watch, shining in the early
   afternoon sun;
awake – the masters are all upstairs selling shares, the kids are
   on the street trading switchblades and nymphos – the trend
   is taking over, the hats are all out

pretty pretty

as long as you've been here, a back ache, the jungle, the E is
   late.
excited for the coast, get these snakes out of my pockets

all
   the working boys
      take 5

eleven dollar juices, thin black girls in diamonds, punting for
   words;
smooth cut backs and make believe bank accounts – revealed

LOS ANGELES

as legacy, marching towards the Pacific – to think of you
smiling, to prepare another urban drag show,
this is the heart, the jungle, the reach around – prepare
yourself.......

the perfect buffalo, the wise palm trees, the glorious beach
– Mark Twain in Hawaii, the sinking opportunity, hauling
school busses across 4th street;
in the wind – drop the pleasantries, grab the books; random
acts of blonde, pretty, pretty
where you been?
where you at?
stick with the plan.

3.

something special for Jesus, across the boulevard, the
California St Germain, the best pickles in the white world;
playing the victim, heartless all over again, mixing juice, the
South Carolina girl smiles;
an explanation (a cautious explanation), a dream to make the
pirates believe;
(i'm a jijitsu starship, i'm a test);
they all come: the Floridians, the Transylvanians, meaning and
tight, grainy t-shirts show the way – a lovely day, while the
universe passes by;
pledging and unanimous – the happiness is speaking in
silence, the price of gas and juice;
splendid, you say.
committed, she replies.
my kingdom for her (HER) phone number;
but you never call, you never wash, you bleached barbarian,
writing kindly so the local surf shop displays your dialogue
–
seemingly the best life ever, spoiled, sleeping on the couch

with a dream and your pants undone;
and you thought it would be forty dollars for the hour........
trim, selective, a fly by, relaxing in the shade, wicked smart,
admirable;
Gilles Peterson running for president, in blue, damned and
adorable.

tisket a tasket.......

her voice echoes across the void: maniac, lover, salesman,
beaming as magic, belonging, tricky, clean red boots with
charm.

she seems nervous

Arjuna steps off the red eye.

and they declare: a hit, a bit of action, cautioned by the
Gods, relevant in cowboy boots, patiently waiting for all
day offshore winds and the mighty mighty to yelp your
name;
gold, weight, frisbee, health, mashuguna - shopaholic, flower
shop debutante, liquor store king, late night addict, public
school pusher, abused - take me out dancing, make me
beautiful - clean and delightful, six foot and glassy, she
ought to find herself a man, she ought to stop and say
hello.

4.

bereavement, over color coordination, explaining visas and
time to any stranger that gets close - elegant and divine,
(DIVINE)

everywhere you go: casual, cool, unemployed, madness, spine

LOS ANGELES

straight and special, as you cringe, as you revolt;
kissing in the jungle, absent of rage, immense - the games the game......

older women smile, lack for nothing, touched, presently
magnificent, you sometime angel, you second story man,
you creepy thespian - the wanting subsides, the voices
mellow, the shoes new;

the Gods they respect you, the sheets are clean, tight jeans
and late payments, milky skin and college tuition due on
the 25th - the modern armory and the homemade granola
bars; pastime defective - memories of thick Latina girls and
the relinquishment of power

"if we love......"

wild! he yells, as he swaggers through the water, demanding
it be natural
respect the natives you read, across the brim of an expensive
trucker hat;
dirty and defensive, all out sensualist, demanding better
service (really.....?);
ah.... reckless, totaled, a short patch of American domination,
a moment of silence for the late Gil Scott Heron

HEAVY SILENCE HERE NOW
....

whatever the ether is doing - thats where we go.

5.

slide into me ether, a hand between your quaking tan thighs,
a longtime memory, a brilliant marketing wunderkid - they

wont wear the hoodies because that Facebook kid made it
famous, and now the older dudes demand resuscitation -
frightened, shaken, (the individual, the green light); play me
a shadow, hold me a demonstration.

"that fuck up put in the first $10 million, but that was it!"

addicted to socks, darker then initially anticipated, gutted,
the models spend the whole day connected, the spirit is
up, distracted, enabled, supported, a nice place to display
this giant cock, with a blushing school girl straight from
boardwalk; access denied, free and fumbling; the West, the
West! burning, with traces of arrogance, with love for the
hazy blue sky, the slight chill in the air, the perfect face
of the girl in a dark wheel chair - those vibrations, those
smiling price tags, those little known Danish artists;
meaning, with a smile, blessed, a surprise when the shaggy
looking bearded blonde boy with the mala beads around
his neck takes a business plan out of his bag and puts it
on the stylish grey stone table for the dude in the cheap
pin stripped button down shirt to flip through - silly
me, thinking you righteous! though we've all been there,
thinking it makes us better, feigning health, afraid of death,
illuminated, clear in the bubble, in love with the
handicapped - the struggle yo, the struggle......

now just practice and do better - (as in the absence of better)
- a sunny urban dream, a photograph to incur the wrath of
Joe Namath; some punk heart, some kale and ginger, some
brown boots and tonic - a bit of jazz, a heavy pour - old
school, piercings and all, so wonderful the style, so fantastic
the shapes!

you can watch yourself while you are eating, she says.

LOS ANGELES

the stickers tell the whole story - everyone gets excited;
  "make no small plans" it reads, through the window,
  outside and heroic, an all cash business, a take home honey
  for the boys to stare at, for the Judas - city plain and sunny,
  hopped up on tainted virgins, trend, blue, new wave
  venture capitalists pushing a stroller, in pink, inside out,
  dressed down (now what you think?) busy, as busy does
  - the whole world runs around and the universe watches
  comfortably and smiles - you push, you push, you push -
  healthy, happy, free, the old Jewish friends from New York
  City who made it big, in love in love in love - "its hard to
  run with the weight of gold;" my tan cheese bag, my light
  vegan holiday.

6.

chasing mommies, cruising in white, basking in the high
  end landscape - the tough girls in beads, with angel wings
  across her back - vibrations and ghetto beats, long distance
  tantra sessions, colorful socks - moving into an upscale
  neighborhood for the alimony.

just another loco getting paid for my vocals;

come sit over here, come purchase me a smoothie;
the daily rancor, the absence of hate, the romance in the
  jungle green (ah, the jungle)

no fuk around, she says.

massive, border jumping, a customs regular - chosen;
take the time, brutal in the absence of honesty and grace,
  branded light, made one - a sprawling garden of dreams
  and temper tantrums - what you heroically call love,
  what you casually dismiss as illegal - obsessed with a giant

smartphone, emboldened by verse, effortlessly fabulous –
you know, you know...... the wind keeps up all day – do
it with love;
ready to go, with the hookers and the addicts, in love with a
hue of green, brandishing a slight smile, behind the wheel
of an American made SUV;

no fuk around

my juice day mama, my jar of kale, my home made poetry,
my bleeding extravagance – take me out for a night, pay
me the big bucks;
another Molotov cocktail please, another brand of chemicals;
purchase power = socks.

you, aware of a trending, ascending society, aware of stars and
light and abdication;
easy with the cash, no worries, all peace, (my Joel Tudor
flashbacks with a single sip);
a mellow corner, a spot in the sun, without the fresh air
you'd be in trouble – immediately local, the long boarders
are going to aim for you, the hacks will call you a star;
my Indian sweetheart, my Ice Cube cell mate;
I've faith in you, she says

yeah?
elevated.
thanks juice!

impressive, creative, the whole family went West, nobody
goes back.
The Abbot Kinney Elevated Bimbo Club (The AKEBC);
The Abbot Kinney Elevated Water Machine (The AKEWM);

last one out, the echo of heels along the shadowed pavement

LOS ANGELES

– my sleeping bag, my Elvis silver coin collection – red and
lovely, the single disaster squad, the two hour work day!
this is my resume, this is my gold coin – a watch for that
verse, a flamingo for that ass

no fuk around

bring in the hot and sour soup, the bass, the X5, the lip ring,
the stripped socks;
bring in the ginger, the hand made sunglass frames, the
mouthy black girls at the shop;
bring in the class wars, the Silicon Alley South Side, the tax
deductions, the agro long boarders; bring in the cool short
twin fins, the fat wide quads, the hot brunettes, eating
Asian vegetables; bring in the laid back security men
talking pork and cocaine

no fuk around

the go hard or go home printing on that gangster's tight
white t shirt, sauntering across the skate park;
bring in the roof decks, the jetty breaks, the homogeny, the
board bag fees;
bring in the jazz bands, the playoffs, the crumbling New York
Knickerbockers;
bring in the sunsets over Topanga, the slack line terrorists, the
metered parking

no fuk around

bring in the expensive hotel rooms, the hookers, the fading
starlets, the short cut jean shorts, the street poets and strung
out Mid Western boys;
(her at the bus stop, her at the zoo);
the shabby chic, the conversation deficit, the smooth

sidewalks

no fuk around

the West Side, the pimps;
anonymous and happy, a cool pair of sneakers to skate in -
 simple living over concrete and sand.

7.

that crazy Polish women on the couch:
i can't tell you about myself, she says sheepishly. If you knew
 about me you would not be sitting here, she says.
but i am darling, i am!
and she knows - the whole do wop, the pick up - just in
 time for Memorial Day......lemons into ginger - just keep
 smiling, he says, its all you can do.

be out of here in a minute if i could, he says. but my whole
 family is here, he continues. can't just desert them.

8.

water.

condemned, a dolphin paddles through the line up as the
 boardwalk looms heavy in the foreground; and outside its
 only ocean, infinite sky, a drop off the deep end, goodbye
 Los Angeles; taken, so clean early, with peaky close out
 waves, mushy and slow early, mushy and slow late.

your engine is dying? she asks with a smile.
no, my engine is fine, he says. that wave was dying.
a smile, a slash at amicability, tight black jeans and all (wait,
 where are we)?

LOS ANGELES

water.

hurled, a smooth right, her shaky bottom turn, her straight
 clean smile and California blonde hair, hunting, sweet as
 dirt, sitting angel - short board and all - consequence is the
 dream, pitched forward, a steady break against the jetty -
 you would stare at her face all day long if you could. a tear
 drop, a seminary assignment, while the kids run wild - into
 it.

a fine way to start the day, he says.

we could be here forever, chained to this chair, this office,
 this choice - everyone is searching for that golden ticket,
 fortunate in that higher tax bracket, verbalizing the
 obvious; the angry black man, who is going to sleep with
 all your white daughters; proper, elegant, the ocean turns a
 bit warmer, her effort, blonde dreadlocks and happy
 - we are only here for a little while, thats what her face
 says, echoing into the morning sky, still charcoal grey
 with a lovely cold - staring out into space, beautiful in her
 simplicity; a rose in all the muck, a smiling face for you
 today, the grains of exhaustive love feels the suns heroic
 rays - an archer in training, a quiet moment (breathing, you
 audible God), puncturing the status quo, called to the
 service of water and charm, bewildered by her easy posture
 - you are really here, you are really receiving her fireside
 invitations;

(a dream, its all a dream)

treat the kids with respect, happy, dancing across the room, as
 light, as hope, a visitor, a small town rebel, treating the local
 girls with kindness;

soft as the music comes on: a lonely harp, a gentle guitar: *the women i'm thinking of, she love me all up…..*

a tiny place in the sun, damp with money (who is going
to control the company?!?), a love posturing, set up as
special, different – the children run wild through the
federal building, abstract in green, preserving, cool with
these Danish shades – the nowness in shoe collections, in
hair color, in job applications – with those colorful socks,
with the incorrigible lightness of gratitude; my little city
in the clouds, when the afternoon sun comes out, pretty
yet serene – how will we do this? how will we continue?
mashed up behind matching black suede high heal shoes –
all the petite Asian girls are embracing the new freedoms of
the Obama Administration……

they cheer for you, they crumble……

a resurgence in dance music, the kids just want to dance
the DJ resounds; patient – patient as a rose (again back
to you), selling the afternoon peace for an opportunity at
celebrity; brash, consumed, shiny – you smooth streets, you
endless construction; you 405, you Wilshire, you Sepulvida
– run, a chance to truly feel the rain, someday, as she drops
into another sneaker shop and is resolutely gone forever
– a memory embalmed in a little poem – the street kids
will certainly laugh it up

sadists

water

in time this precious body melts away and this touch remains
ephemeral – and the mix tapes recover their position,

LOS ANGELES

fantastic, fantastic;
accompanying the abused clocks and unfortunate Gucci
 darlings to the animal executions - take a number.

water, part time yet rich; how are those pictures off the pier?
 promised glory yet retreating behind trend and
 ambivalence - humble, a few moments to dispel the urban
 hostility, the manic assumptions, the older English ladies
 and older tattooed hipsters eating cookies and checking
 their LinkdIn accounts - when do the girls show up? when
 does the trash arrive?
not a travesty, perfectly manicured sidewalks and no smiles,
 ambling around with the same anxious ambivalence that
 destroyed Rome;
particularly brave when doing less; playful with all the
 nostalgic valley girls who listened to your songs in
 high school; learning the music, completely elevated and
 sufficiently massive - your co-workers have all decided to
 dress down, truly independent, creative, bold and Bukowski
 esque - hike those shorts up a bit more, we've been
 patiently waiting here forever.

there is the distinct possibility that no one will show up;
 awaiting the porn girls and Catholic School degenerates;
 pampered in pearls, a memory for French Camila, for
 extremism, slinging peace and development at the creative
 spirits of fat girls and jealous boyfriends; posing for joint
 mug shots behind the Venice Liquor Store, where that hot
 Indian girl used to work;

everyone looks, everyone wonders - at the precipice?
 navigating the expectations of modern literary criticism in
 the digital age - the teenagers have taken over - good.

water

Lightning Bolts and Disco Girls

please sacrifice another mortgage (so prime!) diligent as
  molasses, sunny yet inconvenienced – your haberdashery
  collection grows, your Saturday night uppers and
  hallucinogenic kale crackers; here we go, here we are;

beauty arrives in all shades, unexpected; (they only care after
  the introduction); pain = dance motherfucker! its almost
  summer – what are you going to do? magnetic in those
  boots, that vintage white lace dress, a proponent of free
  love and taxes, in a generation of monsters and saints,
  developing from mud, from gunfire, from the manicured
  excretion, sold in jam jars, for eleven dollars!
cruising in color, such fun, my car is electric.......the sun
  pops in and out, in love with a local girl; that will be the
  tombstone epitaph.

glorious, unbound, your pink mohawk, your afternoon
  glamour, peering into the void (now tri colored) and
  wondering how to pay next months rent.

a divine talent, a radio star; get into it son! this ain't Wall
  Street.

water

a fantastic pestilence, calm under the moonlight, waiting for
  the evening juice session – devoutly transcendent – the kids
  have all the power; open that door for her, magnetic
  and free – across the boulevard, down the corner, hungry,
  metastasized into a diamond; gravy bru – all gravy.

water, even for the young girls.

LOS ANGELES

9.

let me pull up my socks and read you something:

?

repeat as necessary – the quills are sticking out from behind her hot pink panties; you tough motherfucker, you plantation worker; a pretty damsel in a red Range Rover, fresh pickles out on the avenue, hot as Sumatra, creaming on the mischief, all in with the boulevard girls, that concrete catwalk – let them have it;

no fuk around, the tighter the better; if she can get down on this then we are all going to Paris for the final Dylan gig – just in time for the fabulous, out of time, the eccentricities are always in fashion – real as the mid day hookers underneath the Whole Foods; real as the steel grey 535's outside the cafe – out of town short term interest wanted, recognizable in the shade – a healthy penchant for dizzy lovers and silent eye fuck promises that last for days;
painfully all, remise and studious – a knife for this downtown mix up, this cranky monkey wrench tittle fight; the divorcees are all walking their dogs before *and* after yoga class.

am surprised there aren't more motorcycles here; surprised at the chasm and the weight; but where else are you going to go? the freedom is tantamount – home is still home – across the bridges, struggling, classic Jewish decision making, the metro sexual boys are just well dressed pussies – now pull down them pants;

exotic with a temper, between a few rivers once removed –

crash, you suck!
they will suck your cock if you've got the time and the
   money.
am interested; your California walk, your new black Tacoma
   pick up truck with the clean surfboard cushions untouched
   on the tail - a beautiful long board, a tremendous blast
   of sunshine - it always burns off, she says, then walks away
   quickly......

timeless, the mid level management delirium, with a used
   Mercedes to prove that you are somebody, and you are!
the happy couple, the first days of summer, unattached and
   demure, wondering if she is looking at you when Pink
   Floyd comes on

did you exchange.....

when you can languish in the cafes all day and perpetrate;
   when you can walk down the street in a cowboy hat with
   a German Shepard on a long leash;
the envy of all the steady metropolis darlings - breath, and
   move into first;
when you dress in glitter and talk like garbage; when you
   molest and steal and donate and cherish; when you press
   into the chasm, refresh, simplicity, demand that its raw, slide
   into first.

its all one.

pretty angel, petty thief romantic - mushi mushi, lipstick all
over the cheap carrot juice champagne glass.

RICHIE
HAVENS

*

All human, the Ghandi moment, the Cadillac shine;
Push through - the smell of cedar, the morning ocean sound,
 crashing; it's warm already, the birds are late to chirping.
Another pound of flesh, so lovely, so perfect, with rocks in his
 shoes, and twin moons hanging low in the brightening sky.
Dusty, fatigued, counseled, illuminated - this ain't no five and
 dime Jack! the theater suddenly screams;
Best just to stay close to the rocks, don't wade in to far, don't
 laugh at the dirty jokes - now we
are
 considered
  free.
The empty fields and crumbling concrete homes, a derelict
 shanty town, and a third eye bleacher seat to view it all from;
Bob and weave - sure she makes you laugh, that's part of the
 test.......
Admitted defeat, sworn to a faded democracy, following Richie
 Havens to the back of the stage, and done.
Henry Castle looks up for a moment, then falls back to sleep;
From the center of the sun, from a strange teenagers plastered
 bedroom;
an afro and a guitar,

    with Mao Tse Tung
        seated in lotus position
            on the warm wood floor

all your secrets revealed......

"got no time for you motherfucker!"

Please pick up some milk on your way home, God says.

Gently wade into the crumbling ocean, with the heroes and the saints; a scholarly duty, a metaphor for breathing; crash - day time, night time, it no longer matters; drowning in universe and rhyme, covered in bliss and filth, a third round derelict, a machine gun funk, again.

'Wake up Jimi! The water boys want to watch you split the atom.'

At the North End Mr Heavy is beating his fists on the kitchen floor, bloody and obtuse, howling at the infinite dilemma, orgasming to the faint tune of strangers.

Take me home, Brussel Sprout tells him flatly.

You know nothing, and then you are just here, Ganesh tells her confidently.

Such a perfect shape, Mr Heavy thinks. Such a beautiful style; life continues to follow the meandering orange line, with all her raspberry jewels, and shallow forgiveness.

(it all lasts forever, she wearily growls)

Cut out and shaken, the Guanacaste trees unhitch the velvet rope and finally you stroll on in,

(ahhhh, to be on the inside......).

Patti Smith is out on the curb, Patrick Ewing is fatally injured, your heroes are all sleeping on the same floor;

Two tickets to Baghdad, please, she tells Henry. One way.

RICHIE HAVENS

Pussy pussy pussy marijuana, Brussel Sprout sings, when the moon fully sinks below the topaz horizon, and the cannibals are all sitting around, sharpening their spears.

Ahoy! Henry howls. I've Ahab's head, right here, in this tattered canvas sack!

The beach road is a sullen production line, the mommies are all stretched out and pissed;
You can have the ocean, or you can have this computer screen – you decide, it can't be both.
So the angels hide the fat and walk over to the North End, because it's slower up there.
Love me more! Love me more! the cheerleaders gesture; a pack of smokes and a pink sarong laid out on the black sand.
Maybe I'll get laid, Sprout tells her distant lover.
Maybe romance is a drunken massacre, Henry replies.
Bargains, shapes, full time employment and candy cane blow up contests;
Look me straight in the face and tell me you feel nothing, she whispers at the star spangled night sky.

Hemingway just got barreled, the kids are taking over.
It's all HiFi and shaved beauty queens – another left, another sack of dirt.
Buddha declined the offer – he went with a six figure deal from the Asians;
Time is tight and the water is warm; fighting for the soul of a small nameless town;
Low on tooth paste and Jesus Christ; aiming high, determined to be great, she softly says.
A street sweeper, a coloring book – you could have been anything, his sullen Father laments, but you keep going down to the beach........

Lightning Bolts and Disco Girls

Henry stands naked at the entrance way to the proposed toll road, as the bulldozers inch closer.
This is your last chance hippie! Bull Connor says mightily into a trusty horn.
After this it's crucifixion!

It's impossible to leave you! Henry yells back.
The pinball machines are so loud in here, he says to himself.
The yellow Tonka trucks casually advance, as Henry sees visions of Einstein and Nixon, reflected in their dirty steel tracks.
Your teeth are like diamonds! Henry yells at the machines and the tumult.
There is no more time for us, they reply. Bring me a modern romance – tell me a story.
Beauty winks her eye and holds Henry tight.
Tonight you are a star, The Oracle whispers in his ear.
Tonight, it's just you and I.
The sand between my teeth, the lasting disappointment in your eyes - you came here for what?
Love, water, poems, and a 12 string guitar - wonder what it's like in Tahiti? wonder what it's like in Oahu?
We could be dancing for many months, so just turn on the disco and get the fuck.......
My little fuck pad in Pecatu, Henry wonders. What will become of all the gold?
It's a star spangled weekend, it's a long term money plan(hemorrhaging); signs, mermaids, all the jealous critters, all the dime store romances - you could be anywhere, you could be hung upside down.

Damned, and all in, Brussels Sprout says to herself. Fuck, it's hot in here.
Nothing a banana shake wouldn't cure, Leopold offers.
Better check the date on this whole idea, Larry Levan

demands.
It's 1974, we are all going to the beach, driving real slow.
Love me longer, Jezzabel demands.
Pay up front, Henry replies.
Tie a noose, Bruseel Sprout suggests.
He would probably fuck that up as well, Leopold concludes.

Henry lingers a little longer then expected He checks his electronic mail, he searches for healthy toothpaste, he buys bananas and sits in the shade, watching the tourist girls stroll by.
Maybe a second umbilical chord, she said to him over the phone. You need something to ensure that this plan remains on course.
You might be able to ensure that this doesn't happen again, Leopold tells him. If you keep waking up like this, then eventually the sky will fall directly upon you.
You must be out of your fucking mind! Henry snaps at them both.
This ain't nothing but a honkey tonk parade, shaded for tropical expectations.

The big guys hire and fire at will – for kicks; but the masters simply let it all pass; one day Pura Vida, one day dirt.
Rich girl late afternoon events and high class jungle dress codes, for the enchanted, for the mongrels.
Fly me to the moon, Sprout tells Leopold. Make me dishonest and shameful.
You pass the time like a lazy cat, expecting the rainbows to wink and smile every time you get a little blue, Henry tells himself.
Better hope the horn section doesn't run away with your girl, with your Water School library card.
Better hope Tolstoy does not come up here and knock you on the knee caps; take away that smile and that drip.

Einstein comes barreling in through the front door.
Fucking kooks! he rails. This ain't summer camp!
He sits in a big black leather arm chair and stares intently at
  the young girls seated across from him.
He penetrates with his cold blue eyes, and silently ponders
  the weary capitalism between them.
If i don't check my email then nothing gets done, Pinky says.
  And I'm the only one on this project! she laments.
Nina Ranjita rolls her big brown eyes, and continues reading
  her glossy Vanity Fair magazine.

And they are screaming, because no one seems to care: "I'm
  so bored with the USA! I'm so bored with the USA!"
Look what you've done, Leopold tells him. A fine mess, and
  no action......
He still hears them chanting: "Im so bored with the USA! Im
  so bored with the USA......!"
He hears her voice, and it just gets worse.
Your own little insane world, Brussel Sprout tells him.
A magnet for every lunatic hot chick with a passport.
But she is special, Leopold confides.
And so is he, Sprout counters.
Better get the facts straight.

All night Henry reads the obituaries and listens to John
  Coltrane. This is paradise, he concludes.
This is the Atom bomb.

Where is the love? Ganesh asks. You heartless motherfucker.
Larry Levan suddenly awakens from a short disco nap,
  bewildered in a barbers chair on Petitangett, and says flatly
  "hit me with those laser beams."
And all the kids get up and run for the nearest waterfall.

Alone, Henry thinks to himself.
We are all alone, Ganesh replies.

EPILOGUE

Mama mama/all the roads I've known/since I first left home.....

Brussel Sprout hikes up her skirt, and rolls into the casino with style, sandy feet and all.
Motherfucker better have my money! she yells at Einstein.
Came all the way from Atlantis, she continues. Head bobbing and cardiac, with a twist, bitch!

Nice and easy, Ganesh tells her. We only have another million years of this.
Get my hand up that skirt! Brussel Sprout orders. It was truly love at first sight.
All my children, Ganesh sings. All my motherfuckers.

Say I wanna do right/all day/woman......woman!

Just breath, Ganesh confides. If I let my foot up from off your neck then all the universe will flow right in; just like i told you - look up there....... its Perseus, Hercules, Athena, Ray Charles, Miles Davis, KRS 1.

Thats all he knows, Sprout snaps. Comic books and skateboards. Now we have arrived here - this paradise with a price tag. Nobody cares, she manages to admit; with or without the transcendentalism.

Larry Levan stands feircly behind a pair of 1200's in a dark and recessed DJ booth. The only light enters from a long

Lightning Bolts and Disco Girls

and narrow window at the front of the booth. On the other side of the window is a dance floor, full now, under vaulted high ceilings, black, with a disco ball the size of a Mack truck, hanging in the middle of the room.

The cieling is an enigma, and shimmers with crystal glitter and cherry red hearts. The crowd sways back and forth, up and down, side to side; here, but not really here, they say in unison. Not a word, not a chance.

Everyone inhales and exhales, simultaneously, in synch with the music, with everything Larry plays.

You are making them happy tonight, Mr Levan, Ganesh affectionately says.
Larry just smiles.

Ganesh bobs her head and taps her feet to the beat; a slight hip shake, she raises her arms, and fully sways to the left, into a deep slide, when Larry drops Bougie Bougie, and the crowd goes insane.

Ain't no thing, Larry says with a wide clean smile.

When the horns kick in, the dance floor erupts. Beautiful bodies go flying through the air; all their arms are raised to the glitter stars – a long heartbreak, a magical naturalism.

Here we go again, Ganesh says, as the horns drop out of the track, then the heavy bass lines are gone, until the whole production seethes high and light, rising up a final time, above the skyscrapers and heavy garbage cans, above the rats and the sand.

Here we go! Larry screams above the music, faintly heard,

and let's it build, just the front end, then the back, until its time.

Larry turns to Ganesh and smiles fully. Ganesh raises her eyebrows mischievously, cracks a wide, close mouthed grin, and nods her black braided head in slow affirmation. Then, without looking back down at the console in front of him, Larry feels the cool silver knobs with his wet finger tips so perfectly, he taps his feet, gives a long curvaceous hip shake (back and forth), and with his gaze still firmly upon Ganesh, he brings back the bass, then brings back the mids, and the whole room feels elevated, as Miss Universe sashes right through.

The wind, the goddess, the mama, and everyone smiles in relief, and everyone dances.

You are a super hero, Ganesh tells Larry.
I'm an ancient lightning bolt, Larry smartly replies.

Lightning Bolts and Disco Girls

PUNK

*

perhaps its possible to puncture my chest with a blunt pencil, she wonders

the reckoning, the pictures of Stockholm; come home honey, leave the gun, break all the glass in case of an emergency, do it yourself, black leather bleeding from the rectum, tied up in Nicaragua, being fed to the helpless sea lions

passing heroin between the garbage can disco (old, old, old), she sleeps all afternoon

reckon she fucked everyone on the beach, he thinks – lonely, high 80's, a bit of wind, clear blue sky, one could see the volcano in the Northern distance, one could hold her glance for a moment then loose it to another sucker, another white idol, lonely and broke – another peace march

the punk stars have taken stock of everyone's lives from the truck parked behind an ever growing fruit stand on the 212; sorting organic mushrooms and helplessly watching the clementines go out of season – its a daily struggle with frost and odors, eager customers and wilting flowers – the trucks are late,

Lightning Bolts and Disco Girls

the mangos require sorting, the register is off again

from elsewhere the sounds of loud guitars, bursting organs,
blinding stage lights and delirious food peddlers. the lead
singer hovers over a burning microphone stand and speaks
in tongues, tears out his lower intestines and makes love
to the standing first row; the hungry high school students
shuffling amid the push and pull, the torn and bleeding
egocentric audience – a bursting of light, a candid vision
of an alternative universe where all the people (little divine
machines) move along as ants upon a hill, from one gig to
the next, on treadmills, life cycles, skateboards, and telephones
– just another galaxy over, then a thousand more galaxies
over, carrying out the same ethos; and eventually we move
onto the next one, another set of rules and tests and random
sexual encounters; and from the front of the stage he beats
us lonely, and recognizes his time outside the box, with an
F chord and a lucrative three record deal; and he is awash in
sunlight, on a beach clean and happy, with no hooks in his
back

A minor; C, G, A minor, F; the retreat of Richard Nixon, the
brass bands lucid elegy for someone special

along the dimly lit streets of Avenue A is the beast, the empty
fire hydrants and porcelain statues of Joey Ramone, breaking
a two decade old truce with the Benjamins, carrying gun
powder in a small black pack through all the downtown
subway stations, ranting about peace and prosperity to
anyone that might listen; she takes the time, believes in him:
harmless, handsome, divine, stretched out naked and alone
and right, building hand grenades and scribbling slow angelic
love songs for the jest set crowd

don't know, he said, just thought that is what you are

PUNK

supposed to do.......

she screams out at the the magenta sky, still reeling from
the mornings news; positive, dying, aching, every morning
up and down five flights of stairs, then nod amicably at the
friendly Italian pervert planting artichokes in the wooden
garden box nestled into the stifling concrete, across from
the ranting garbage cans; rich and unhappy, with a healthy
savings account and two boys in college on the West Coast,
because 'that's where the easy girls are'

you have to deal with this now: rotting, from the inside out,
and not in the daily spiritual way but the disintegrating
spoiled cabbage death; of the Brooklyn cyclone rotting, the
towers rotting, the black cat hell race rotting; for all that
greasy sex and those magnificent loose nights, just to feel
new, young, just to feel something

punk

the final infiltration arrived in the dark, at the bottom of a
damp staircase; the yearning, the end of something, a new
life, whatever his name is, where ever we are, just thinking
this: trust him for the best, in all that grime, in all that heavy
climax disaster, pointed steadily at the protruding moon and
foreign capital cities

punk

the lonely walk along the beach road is pretty in sliced rags
and empty pockets, the soles of her new flip flops coming
undone, past the green cemetery and downed trees since the
earthquake

to the beach, just in time to see a hot pink bikini butterfly,

Lightning Bolts and Disco Girls

with a long needless stride across the sand towards the ocean
– this is for all of you, this is for none of you, she whispers;
and the disco lights turn on, and the metal detectors come
to life, and the magnets are swimming around George
Clooney's lap pool, just before the pre release party of
something fabulous

she is rotting inside, infected, deterred, keenly aware of her
position in this life, of her rising fate

from the crackling radio next to the bed, in another cheap
pay by the hour motel room: found dead in Spain, in what
the local authorities are calling a crime of passion; at the steps
of the Washington Monument waiting for some one pretty,
anonymous, able; sipping from a dirty plastic thermos hustled
from a distant home; with her hat pulled down low and a
scarf around her bruised neck; someone to smile at, to be
honest with, to take the pain away......

you are here alone? he asks
yes, i am here alone, she answers

he moves closer into her, and she thinks of chaos math, as
his fingertips touch her narrow cleft chin, and then suddenly
his lips are upon her, in the open air, in America, with the
President and the First Lady close by, and the Supreme Court
around the corner; he touches her breast over an expensive
leather jacket, and when she lets him, she re affirms his
suspicions, while on the side walk a small family from France
snap photographs of the 21st century prestige, the debacle

later a breeze enters the room and she pulls the sheet up over
her naked body; she is alone in the room now, thankful he is
gone, and she is empty again – no one to explain it all to, no
one to deceive; we are all infected now, she thinks, watching

PUNK

the ceiling fan spin on a medium setting, and she turns on
the radio next to the bed and listens to the news reports in
Italian, and then jazz music soft and slow

this is how i shall die, she thinks, and closes her eyes again,
falling back into a shallow sleep

punks

along the train tracks, hoping empty box cars; destitution
and benevolent progress collide in Central America, where
no one really knows, where everyone is just getting by – the
liquid holiday, the dark purple umbrella plants, the all day
tours around the block; centrally located, dramatic, as the
morning clouds recede and a blue sky arrives again, and the
ocean hums against a small island of sharp rocks down by
the beach, where the pretty white girls get hurt and the boys
don't know what to say

everyone is bloody

rowdy, down Houston Street, then across the bridge, then
back across the bridge again; she started as a coat check girl,
then started fucking the head bartender, then was moved
to the rear ticketing booth, then gave head to both security
men at the side entrance (at the same time) and was fired
on the spot for negligence, then hired back again to cocktail
a private fundraiser for The Captain, where a celebrity
boy band played a short set, and there were balloons and
champagne and vegan cookies

the tattoo above her shaved vagina reads 'never forget', in
Hebrew

the silver haired pop stars, the matching long legged

dilettantes, priceless, masturbating, happy all night long, just waiting for her to call – all the kids are turning colors, all the shoes are on sale; she breaks her neck trying to play someone elses bloody introduction, a few chords to a song she wanted to write for him; and she thinks 'amnesty now, fuck the low paying literature jobs.'

PUNK

★ Part *three*

THE MUSE

For S.S

*

1.

the muse is a bitch, the girl ain't nothing but trouble......
a dragon tattoo across her fanny, a sharp tongue for all the
   modern lovers.

2.

the muse is a bitch, in flip flops and cut away t-shirts, ragged
   green shorts, eyes dark as dirt.
not so sweet, she says, and stares off into the darkness;
out there voices, out there the void, the newspapers and
   hardware stores,the Bob Dylan bootleg albums and dime
   store hussys;
out there its wild water blue and yellow polka dot sunshine
   forever.
dark skin, homesick for years, so young and elegant, so sharp
   and alarming;
with ragged master plans, a sexual deviant in the afternoon,
   laying around hung over and bored,
its cultural suicide, its a natural disaster.

she arrives at the beach with a smile and slices you to pieces;
the muse is a barreling plot of existence, with curves, coy and
    plotting:
a midnight heist in Las Vegas, a new redwood forest.
falling asleep in a hammock under the open blue sky roller
    coaster – all the longboards are out front, all the
    majesty.......
balancing a mystic life and a dirty career, from one paradise
    to the next, throbbing, burning, alive, taking pieces of the
    dream (a six string and a head wrap),
makes all the young boys swoon.

3.

small surf town paradise, the wind is offshore, the longboards
    are out.
marching towards the sun – the ecstasy, the farce, the wind;
Woodstock on the side of a cliff – a job, a purpose, a
    penetration.
beauty arrives, dark skinned and unannounced, sweet and
    smiling, curious:
what heroes are here? what secrets to be held?
elegant, nature toiling, all this water, uncommon amongst
    thieves, the pleasant pastime for sweethearts and lovers;
the endless reef Serpico action, the hippies and ex presidents,
    the idle conversations in foreign languages;
the quiet village at mediation time, the sweltering days with
    nothing to do but stare out at the sea;
maybe this is finally home, she secretly wonders.

finally, a disco girl beauty, ragged and hot, slinging beads
    and necklaces (dark blue, threaded together with green and
    turquoise, similar to a tropical sea),
while the boys paddle out to the catamarans and drink cheap
    beers in the hot sun, and the girls are peckish on the beach,

THE MUSE

   comparing love affairs and groovy vacation crushes.
the crashing star sits idle in his beach side cafe, smoking
   Drinking jamu, draped in colorful sarongs, tanned and
   messy, indifferent and protective;
mami, star child, flower girl, madame, passing the time
   peacefully, this bloody home, he says to himself.
maybe it's over, he wonders; the liquid diligence, the round
   inferno of the sun,
they all tattooed, all messy, wild, with expired visas, and no
   money to return home;
modern heroics and warm water suicides, as the artists sit on
   the beach staring endlessly at the horizon, wondering what
she might be doing now.

4.

suffer!
suffer from the heat and the sky
suffer from the air and the night;
suffer from the silence and the fucking
suffer from the shapes and tides;
suffer from the plain bread and water
suffer from the island's rumbling glow.

5.

the modern romance: slinging cool head nods while passing
   along the stairs,
on the edge of a liquid razor blade, small talking sports and
   girls, gazing at the light from a monster setting sun, quiet
   and alone in the crowd, secretly hoping for survival, the
   beating heart and mellow glance, all poor, all here, all time,
   (she has a face that makes you cry, and the attitude of
   broken glass).
the lady lovers and smooth salt water hustlers pass down the

line;
sometimes its difficult to turn, to balance, where there is
   music and light, and you have cheated her again, and you
   have regained your sense of loss.

all the young white girls act so hard, all the boys are looking
   for cash;
$1.50 for a loaf of bread, common Buddha survival tactics
   means forever water.
the honey gangsters down at the beach for sunset spin fuck
   you tales for the depraved love children, while around back
   its electric Jimi Hendrix star life for one hand clapping.
up the stairs and its silent (no audience, no troubles) as the
   cathedral roars to life, as the spray touches the back of your
   neck.
bliss, long distance lovers and no electricity bills,
and the Gods yell "trendy is not good, make sure it works!"

6.

its a long walk back to Manhattan, its a lovely night to kiss
   her.
the only things that is real happens out there, in the ocean,
   she laments; everything else is a mirage.

the muse is a bitch, a familiar love song, a dirty pair of socks.

DELANCY STREET AND THE GUN

*

If you just believe, she said, hovering, covered in cash and muck.
This you just believe, she said, panting, half naked, revealed,
   Sitting on the white tile floor, cool in the early morning.

The chances - hide the drugs, pay the girls, walk over the rocks;
Amnesty, ghetto child, a make believe hypocrisy, breathing just
   to make sure.
Special, often tangled; just believe, she said, and cupped her
   hands around her heart, and evoked the story of her father,
   her temple, her child, her eyes welling up with water, and the
   frosting of night (penetrated) slowly passes.

A stranger, another monster.

The sun is hot, burning, with the open fields and curving blue
   horizon;
Take chances, live fully - you swell in exhaustion, admiration,
   new loves and daily routines;
A straight answer, an empty boat hunting for that rainbow
   colored whale.
You are quiet, she says, then tries to extort more money from
   the amateur pimp.

It's a hard and lonely job, it's wild and burning, from up on
   Delancy Avenue,
From the coastal towns that bare her name and memory;
Welcome to the big city, now everybody just relax, you
   cautiously stammer.

Spending the time and money, lightly delirious, the entire
   body tingles with slipping dreams and hot dangerous
   affairs, with strangers and devotees.
Come a little closer, get out of that room, line up for the
   master;
Your friends come and go, yet no one else really seems to
   mind.

Rhythm, price gauging, monolithic failures and grand intent,
   peering out the side window, listening to reggae in order
   to make the darkness pass;
Leave the doors open so we can air out the crumbling
   monastery, the last virgin in a heap of trouble, with one eye
   on the gun, and the other on the karma;

With one eye on the gun and the other on the karma.

The percentages are rising – it takes four wandering
   butterflies to inspire a poem;

Here, out on the cross, maintaining the slight semblance of
   reason, morality, hope, the dream slithers in and out of the
   living room, waiting for the tides again;
The heavy funds of rock and roll, the total obsession with
   style, makes the body rest, makes the bedrooms empty and
   dear.
Solace, their names are unknown and blind – she speaks, of
   faith and Gods and buildings.
Just believe, she says, as the music gets louder, as Jimi Hendrix

DELANCY STREET AND THE GUN

prevails.
A life raft for this sinking island, for this squandered self
   esteem (the silent benders, the late night city runs, the
   punk focus and dedication to tribe,
Elevates the soul, and keeps the pretty girls coming back for
   more).
What's her name? What's the difference.

The water, the gun: what's the difference?
She gets in the car, with all that dirty cash close to her chest,
   fixes her hair in the window, and prepares for the next sale,
   for the next crucifixion.

dost though love life? Then do not squander the time, for
   that is the stuff life is made of.

A heavy dose of reality, a moment outside the jungle;
Her long sad face, stuck in it – a slave, a burden, prepares for
   battle once again.
It's heavy out there; it is elegant, and homicidal.

Do you believe? she asks.
The memories come flooding in, first of water, then of air,
   and finally trees and open valleys
(that magical dwelling atop the hill);

He screams and plays,
He wilts and rises.
Believe! she wails,
Across the stretched worn skin of the drum,
Across the straining dance floor and infinite wave;
This is it, this is fabulous, perfect, love; this is everything!
Now get in the car!

You spend the best time in peace, in practice – observe the

simple ecstatic courage in doing.
Fanatical *and* easy going – a revolution, a cult figure;
Do a bit of this, the pressures are all basic – light up Times Square, ponder the Earth;
"better to live a single day in freedom then a life in slavery," or something like that.......

The chants of free men, of gratitude – the smell of sage, the meaning in that sliver of grass, perpetuating the sex slave economy, driven mad with envy;
Proper regards for that bubble in the sky, kind farewells for the burdens and doubt.
She moves around the room, speculating what might become of it all;
If we keep dancing, if we keep paddling, if we gaze onto the sun and feel that original warmth upon the skin, then all is not lost, then all is not blind.

The chants of free men, across Delancy Street, heart on the trigger and sweat on the brow;
Darling darling, downtown and up, thankful and swelling, dirty and smiling.
Play that 6 string daddy, whisper that poetry.
Huck huck, go go.

THE BUTTERFLIES ARE MELTING

*

1.

Easy, windy, grace, pastime promise, then empty, then gone;
Legitimate - you bring that heat back, you tear open the chest;
The food is spicy, the fraternities are deep - so in it, so
   drowning.

Another wait - the horizon is pink and blue and grey, swirling
   - this could last forever, Lakshmi memorabilia and wealthy
   cups of ginger tea.
The Westerners are safe under the bright lights, with light
   acoustic music playing, and various bottles of imported wines
   empty on the steps.
The moon has reached her pinnacle, fat and smooth, the
   toothless giant, the man - yes, yes, yes, here again.

How are the islands? he asks.
Ya know,......he slowly reply.
All the Lower East Side drama, all the heavy water - a longing
   at 3rd Avenue, for the disco Bowery, the Bukit lights, the
   heroin divas, the salt water sugar mamas.
This is how you jail.......you've been thinking too much -

fastest way to trouble and erosion, expressway to dirty girls and bi polar power couples;
Alas, the queen is going back to sleep, and you rip and rip at the void (helpless giant), the simple job is to go bigger (a jungle realization, and now you know).

The butterflies are melting, the traffic is back in style.
Professional hippies, that is what Francios called them; and now he sits and drinks and is among them – Treme sell out, supermarket king, thrift store debutante, meat market terrorist;
Ka-boom! *And if you don't know now you know......*
Taciturn two steps with an acid flash dance angel, muling small plastic baggies of cheap blow through Singapore – the loud speaker trembles, the earth stops moving.
Whatever makes you happy – whatever makes you smile;
Feel that rage, her name is jealousy, her name is lust, her name is hate – breathing compliments and inviting disaster.....at least you have a job, at least you got her phone number.

Hati hati – the water girls put on their black jackets and order the half portions.
Come over here and remind me of that taste – as the party girls call up another wet dream, and the muscle boys just stand around smiling.
Blessed the dream – blessed the ocean and her rolling nymphs;
Just a simple case of dehydration, just a comfortable corner to write poetry from.
Earth calling mama, earth calling mama – so young and able, such a virgin at 37 – been hijacked and handled, spraying about my last barrel......
To the moon! To the moon!
Andy Kaufman look alike contests and butterfly

concentration camps by the sea; enter here.
Kook, wild, a clear pool of blood, a strongly hung hammock
to watch the apocalypse from;
Hati hati – it's cake and cookies for all the Peninsula lust
addicts, and their nonchalant glances;
Pick up the tab, keep the hot water coming.

Survival:
It's all so fucked, Einstein admits. No one believes that I
can do this from a house.
Some French dude came over here the other day, and he
didn't know what he wanted.
'Maybe a fish, maybe a longboard......'
Ahhh, get out of here, Einstein tells him. You can't even
surf!
A few dirty pictures, then she doesn't write back;
Dressed to impress, all up in gravy;
Punk ass bitches, those dragon tattoos, bleeding out in style,
with all the aristocrat runaways.
A fingertip all the way up her thigh, a melody to remember
your name – satvic suggestions soothe all the beautiful
heavy girls on a cruisy Tuesday night;
Strong as a cabal, testy as a promise – missing Francious at sea
level – rolling.
Mary Mary, why ya buggin?
A late night highlight reel, a modern obsession for the
destitute mermaids, and all of Ahab's merry men;
There will be pearls at the end of here, they tell you.
The Gods stand around, amused at your attempts to stand up;
Just wasting time and practicing a smile.......
Seriously though, what's your name?

Lightning Bolts and Disco Girls

2.

- Punchy, because you can be – a lost soul, a memory, from the hills to the blank waters edge, and all the ferocious roads between Winamuka and the Upper West Side, wrapped in jungle, on the down low, for the mini skirt long board girls;
- The first seed in a long line of insane poetic Hungarians, drunk on ginger and flexing at strangers – peace, a bit more love, a bit more tender boogie woogie, a bit more water please.
- The blades of grass have been over exposed and socially networked;
- The police are coming, you sexy motherfucker, you focused Nazi wet dream, you free bastard, you penny at the bottom of a dark and endless well;
- You sexy motherfucker, suave in red, getting closer, wanting another dagger, another hit and run, patiently watching the nuclear fall out, the last view of Ellis Island from an expensive seat – hello skybox, hello luxury, hello girls!
- Massive, cut and infected, the warrior in a box, constantly sending love, obscure and erect, never knowing when she might show up, when the mood suits her, when the band goes back on;
- Surely she fucked all those Brazilian boys while out on Lombok – hello threesomes, hello medicine.
- A legend, coming around again....the fact is that the big dudes get all the cash and pussy – light musings and fake Hermes bags; entry level price wars and progressive antics, just for a mermaid, just for a cover up.

Intensions, breaking, always, the blue skies and tropical fairy tales – so far from here, so wonderful in the light – another poet, another swing – you've been here before, the sharp edge, the stolen diamond, as the music gets lower, as the

THE BUTTERFLIES ARE MELTING

tables clear out, and still the heavy breaking, the marching orders, straight at Paris - yet still she doesn't know her trajectory, her fleeting purpose - *It just doesn't matter! It just doesn't matter!*.

3.

Punctured, lit up, obviously to want for nothing, as still the dream contracts and expands, a brief wedding dance, a synthesizer and a razor blade - you heartless bastard, so well trained; out and back, real slow, just the way he would have wanted it - come closer, get over here, imagine she is there for you, her in gold, her in vines, birthing apples, blending the family business, all for the cash, all for that walk.

Again: hati hati - take me back to Manhattan and kill me, please don't let me die here.....
I'm gonna fuck you up! he scowls, and the German Shepard barks, and tears apart another African genius; but nothing comes close - a slight erection, an elation, another sentence please, wailing at the moonlight, all the gangster menage and well lit speak easys - I wonder if Plato is spinning tonight - more poison please.

Dedicated to Marvelous Marvin Haglar...

She has the monopoly on small talk; such tension, such passion, such dedication - pronounced Aikau - don't fuck up.
A mellow night on the farm, a busy night on the Peninsula, a stolen credit card in case you need to get a ticket out of here - such a crashing angel, such a manic darling - wet constantly, just grab on and go.
From where ever you are, from the floor seats at The Garden;
Outside in the rain, praying for more time, elastic and screaming 'in you, in you!' the best place ever, the mature

thing to do......
Dedicated to Lester Bangs - a fresh dose of courage, a long night of melting - cracked, pseudo intellectual, high end hippie, long term hipster, practicing, chewing on ginger and pussy;
"The champ is here! The champ is here!"
Better bring that sugar, better open them arms - a rolling stone, a city kid rambling along the oceans hungry edge;
Dedicated to the legends, that cut South African, and the wandering hostess in red

(always in red).

ENGLISH
LESSONS

*

flirt, the alley way blues, the profit, the masquerade and the
   whore;
lost, a holy virgin at 17, wild since 23, blind and gagged since
   last night;
the last ferry out, the marvelous soul singer and ginger night
   intrigue - pick me up someone special, lay it all out in honey;
missing, it *and* you - a trust fund holiday and a paper chase
   lingerie party to tell papa about, before the breathing stops;
simple pleasures, merry mockery, we chased waves and women
   together, we laid it all out in blue;
per me, swallow harder, penetrated and worn - what no one
   else asks, what the girls dictate;
hurry up and go, take the other half of that pill, sprawled out,
   naked and sunburned, on a dirty pair of floral patterned
   sheets, in a crumbling three story motel in Asia (been there,
   done that), when she finally shows up, all dressed in red.

it stings, it hurts, a little bit, shallow and quiet - another freight
   train, a special coin - drifting, and the honey just left the
   room, and the sugar just tipped over;
viral, savage, menage - a fuck bag and an ounce of chronic -
   Tuesday night on the Bukit, flying the red eye - dry mouthed

and unbelievable, made up in lace, vulgar in cherry, the last
time you decided to call, the cum stains on the high thread
count sheets;

dirty without a forecast, blessed in salt and grime - another
wicked shorty, another drowning late night sex talk;

oh, the more you want the more you burn, the greater
the risk - out comes the chains, in comes the hustlers -
bittersweet, with a cleaver, a dirty syringe, an impatient
lover, a drowning soul;

full time masochist, every day hero - butchered, living with
the whole New York City skyline in the burning distance,

allowed to survive, wanted as hero, demanding more pay and
another fuck bag to take over the bridge (only if she
answers the door);

pretty pretty, voluptuous and sound, melting, slowly, late
night, the ginger high, a hammer and a lot of nails...... true
love, as the evening songbirds float through a warm night,
and invite all the loose debutantes around, for the Italian
girls who take all the hot boys home;

death, the final round, the impressive farewell - come home
with me, waiting, a knife and a rubber - sweat dreams
Mephistopheles, it feels better this way.

best just to watch the space between her legs......

its all in the lips; a rose, a fee - goodnight angel, welcome
back darling; when it all turns to rage,

when it all leads to anguish - firm in filth, full in passion, a
furious storm of bullshit eccentricities and revolving dues -
how do they perform so cold, inside and out, alone at
night, listening to the motorcycles go by;

what would Miller do? what is that beating sound?

a similar surprise, another heartbreak, born of emptiness and
wet shards of glass, fucked and happy in the midnight
temple;

she is plump and beautiful - she is a relic and shinny - bound
by bitterness and orgasm, dreaming of penetration all day

long, then reserving tables and hustling, the latest island
fashions under the stars, with the wilting sound of jazz and
small town gossip;
the easy entry, the hard to get at, major and sublime, forever
adorned in red and white, gliding across the floor - an
intellectual stab at service, and love - you look so elegant
and strong, controlling the whole situation, Stalin with the
lights off;
there is nowhere to be and no one to see - all the party girls
are in the back, and the band plays lazy and sad - at least its
cool, at leasts its not raining.

the dream is the tragedy, further drowning into that fantastic
dilemma, daily and nightly;
your well pressed suits, those trim red dresses, the long
sinuous smiles that mean nothing - torturous and churning
- forever, thats your password, with a sledgehammer and a
dream.

she passes again, the stars are always dancing, the glasses of
champagne and bloody reef scars, perform two shows per
night, every night;
above the cliff the young girls are contemplating a new dive;
come here, with kisses and long late night hugs, bending
over, always on stage, skinny and beautiful, a rose for your
secrets, a handshake for the cash;
short haired and tattooed, a motherfucker, certified - this
is where the fun begins, engaged with indecision and
hormones - which one is for me?
(my father was into socks, and now its my turn);
hereditary disfigurements, the space between the circle, the
burning, the party......certainly the new girls remember
you, and the swine eaves a dirty message on the shower
door, begging or another taste.
the currency is growing, and the hippies are getting all

Lightning Bolts and Disco Girls

    dressed up – its Sunday night, its time to play;
the generous French women, elegant in gesture and touch,
    seething with colloquialisms of love and fashion, beat on
    the Bukit, and beyond – a short lesson in kissing, a strong
    touch to convey the problem – here we are, the princess
    and the charioteers, come love us and our wet dirty
    whoring ways;
just what you came for, just what you dreamed it would be.

The American curse, the love at first sight litmus water
    test;
like ships in the night, you say, all out of proportion and
    heavy, close to the sand, watching water gently rise and roll
    onto the beach, with the tasteful delight of weary gypsy
    love and astral longboard sweethearts;
the freedom intoxicates, falling into your thin tan arms,
    awkward and silent, destined for greatness, purged of the
    small conflicts related to taste and worry, dwelling in the
    outer reaches of Gods and war, battling for a better spot in
    the line up, cursing strangers for selfish reasons, elated to
    still be in the exhaustive moment of touch and gaze – here
    we are, here we go;
maximum push and pull, from the maniac who can sing The
    Gita and drink like a fish;
from the complete element of savior, rich and listening to
    wind and sand, favored by the angels and the whole
    celestial gang;
from the last stop on the A train, the tie dye sarong around
    Buddha's bulging neck (we know nothing);
in the beautiful silence, in the early afternoon – thanks for
    coming, welcome to the show;
absent of maladies, soft with a condom, full in spirit, erect
    in action – patience, while all the pretty girls decide which
    direction to go (all so wonderful, all so dying).

ENGLISH LESSONS

- She is frantic, high, radiating through life and time, skipping from one lover to the next, perfect for the elevated pirate and metaphysical diamond trader;
- cool, as hero, as marksman, as prey - represent the stars and the rolling glory of home and business - how are you today? where are you from?
- the colors are a turn on - the hippies are dialing home, the increased numbers promise possession and stress - just being, just sitting.......
- just back from Nepal, en route to India, learning to surf, impossible to own, easy to chase - all the modern defects, all the classic attractions - ecstasy, staying till the first set ends;
- the masters and their tools, the harpoon makers and their caskets;
- double on the ginger please - let me run these thick scratched hands through your hair, marvelous smile and mysteriously content - an artist, an athlete, a star, blue in the early morning, with color and style, as the sun gently comes out, and the breeze passes through the open jungle streets;
- isn't love grand - are we having fun yet?
- in and out, everyday, the impossible turn, the butterfly sensation;

just like music........

- a constant rhythm, that hair, that smile, those legs......a day full of suffering, till she appears again;
- again, the full, the simplicity, the canon of love and spirit and wine parades around the beach, naked and erect, thoroughly ready to show up, appreciate and drown, in the falsetto voice, in and out of story, rhyme (another) and vice (this is what we talk about), cured of all rejection, injected with faith, grandiose in dream and mouth (such full lips!)

Lightning Bolts and Disco Girls

as the managers attempt their erotic stories and the bra
boys slip into a coma.

conscious, her plan as an artist, a figurehead, a sex star,
  following the call of the body, the pandering appetite, the
  insatiable hunger, pulsing, pulls her close, straddles the
  chair, walks slow and speaks with deliberate punch,
  intention, grace, with swipes at tenderness and affection
  (can one trust such beauty?), confident for the crowd,
  isolated for the legacy (*she got everything she needs.....*),
  the flowers are raw, dead, and perfect;
appreciate the moment, the delivery and presence, as karma,
  as a gift from her soft full lips and thin delicate hands,
  worried about tomorrow and running from yesterday,
  awash in the sorrows and euphoria of charged living (the
  tight rope, the drama), portraying the princess hero, the
  warriors courage, the adolescent desires – and again her
  lover, her touch, her laugh, with sand between her curled
  baby toes and diamonds in her piercing samurai eyes;

and in conclusion, from the dirty financial districts to the
  placid cool mountain plains, with honest speech and
  careful hands, leaning in slightly while the music plays,
  with a pause, gaining intension, you say "everyone just
  wants to be loved," and with a nod you both agree and
  watch the girls pass by, and all the tables full of lunatics, and
  the wine cellar locked, and the stars all out and free.

So beautiful, so in and out, with a feeling (blessed) and the
  sun soaked deliverance of morning, awake, unbound, the
  theory of ocean and song, melodic as the tide rises, and the
  bikini mountain top appears;
dinners with computers, with gorgeous drones, with
  international stars – between celebrity and absolute
  obscurity, gesturing fuck at the alley cats and muscle bra

ENGLISH LESSONS

   bra lynch mobs;
peace and happiness, delicate and grand, hey hey, the black
   has arrived, the purple is on the way, the pretty girls are
   happening, the house is silent – in times of war, of great
   privilege, of Warholian standard, of Churchill and color,
   professional and kind, humble and tired, beat up again, the
   angel, the obsession, the fanatic, the lesser of all evils,
   pushing, as a dreamer, a tattoo on the open wrist, a bass
   head and a broad to bring home for dinner; they nap all
   afternoon and party all night – perhaps a quick surf at
   sunset, enough cash to make it back from the beach –
   prophetic beauties, sun soaked angels, foreign show girls,
   indecisive and drunk on freedom, tantamount;
she lets the tattered black t shirt slip off her shoulder as she
   rocks back and forth on her heels and acts innocent for
   water logged suitors and expatriated love toys;
only the best, you say, ascending to innocence, lost in poetry'
   recollecting bigger waves, astounded by death;
"we're all from Denver," he says flatly. "you're in Denver!"
so beautiful, again her full lips, her backwoods sensibility,
   her Parisian counterparts, attempting to enter island
   civility, sophisticated sunshine patriotism with her
   meticulous shabby chic partnerships and dismayed
   lover, imprisoned by her beauty and soft allusive speech,
   wondering of artistic endeavors, money and history;
across the dinner table, lit by a single hanging light bulb,
   asking about organisms and travel itineraries (where ya
   been? where ya going?), with tan skin, long full brown hair,
   thin sunken shoulders and a full strong neck – the fairy tale
   type, butterflies, alive and crawling around the table, to lay
   a palm on her inner thigh and around the back of her
   head, through the hair, full of blind intension and milk;
erect easily (just being around her) as the evening light fades,
   just for the moments, a raw accumulation of sorrows and
   heartbreak and simple wet euphoria, inspired by a setting

sun and a silent wind - you have it now, falling from the
moon, adrift in blue, passionate, (devoutly), picking sections
and craters, to mourn her presence and die in her absence;
let's speak of paintings, of film, of awkwardness and defeatist
mentalities - *you* can be anything! you long to scream
at her, generous as kin, loose as Hollywood - the pastime
promises, the strange boys whom all desire her kind touch
and heavy lips - they line up now, at the Warungs along
the beach, someone to take the edge off, to make sense
of it all, after sunset, right before death, inhale, feel the cold
(cool as water) and drop into the void again, as she laughs,
and laments your sloppy affections (not supposed to fall in
love).

its a staunch evening, a serious endeavor, perfect on the
deck of the Pequod, outside in Woodstock, lost in Byron
Bay, bitchin in Bali (all those colorful fashions, all those
thin business cards), with the music turned up loud and
water boiling and the body cold and the soul reckoning
another muse, another adventure (no comparisons, no
questions);
soon we are off for G land, for Sumbawa, for Senegal, for the
New York State Thruway;
packed and happy, leaving the lovers and friends, apparently
rich, shameless yet humble, with less time, daily hounded
by indecision and pause, compassionate and concerned, yet
still greedy, and bulging with lust and infidelity,

oh world, oh light!

turn around, bend over, obey the beast, dance a little more -
the beauty again, the aligning stars and spiritual
indentation, *house music, it's a spiritual thing* the radio
howls, confirming truth and gesture and glide - your
perpetual glide and everlasting drops - she paints another

masterpiece *(be, simply be)* and vanishes into the night -
an angel, a teardrop, a disciple - hello butterfly, hello lover.

Goodby butterfly, goodby lover.

EPILOGUE

the waste is enormous, overwhelming, creates paralysis and
   inspires nightmares, while in the water everyone waits for a
   whale that may never come.
she is fantastically alone - the self imposed Alcatraz
   afternoons, with a village walking up and down the steep
   stairs, bound by glamour, rolling, blissed out and burning
   - amok in creation and envy, thundering through the latest
   sustainable fashion trends, with black hands and delirious
   smiles (I'm losing my mind, she whispers), while her most
   recent lover searches for his shoes, and trips over the
   crystals.
won't they ever leave? won't there ever be peace?
from inside, a heart and a flash, the personal Nagasaki, the
   bleeding, the Berlin hangovers, up all night for no good
   reason, working on another poem for no one special -
   delicious and decomposing;
in the morning the ocean calls, the head throbs, the body
   cries - and the beach watches you paddle into the horizon
   - another time perhaps, another life maybe.

the simple reasoning - what you are dedicated to, what you
   adore.......come and go, come and go.

★ Part *four*

C O O L

For S Peshy

*

Cool slide, straight out the back, who's your daddy now? Didn't know you cared.
All tied up and pretty - the cuffs are tight, you say - this is forever now;
You and that jiggle jiggle cadence, clean and antidotal - so beautiful: the curl, the mellow drop;
Hard when it is small, precise and permanent, the heavy branches from the tree, the silent lotus flower, her divine offerings.....
Close the eyes, look with all the light and grace - there is Guruji, there is Gerry Lopez;
Smile, all we can truly do.

Henry has gone filandering, the party girls are just warming up, the boat boys are grieving;
haven't had a good one yet, Paul Newman tells Brussel Sprout;
With the sun shinning bright and the water warm; a tiny spec in the universe, a mini cosmos, a moment along the beads of time,
(it's just the moments that we really get, Brussel Sprout says, laconically);
With the red roses and blue horizon, as far as you can view;

Chill, loving, the moments of peace, above the oceans edge,
   but you can still hear it:

Be cool, she whispers; I'm with you forever now.

H A R M L E S S

*

INTRODUCTION

Great: dear blooming, pounding sea – a window left open, a
   dull light across an endless horizon.
The fates and lures of the special case, the naked woman, the
   yearning sea,
(but she successfully yearns for nothing......).
The morning and her sharp wit, her favorite passing cloud, her
   ancient designs;
arrive here, where concrete dubiously meets the rock, and
   pay double, from empty pockets, for the sprouting yellow
   buttercups, and the foolish pink rose.
With a slight wisp of wind, a fortune of words, a ragged sack of
   poem and song,
the great
     celebrity status
      thankfully slips away, as the kind wet earth
        welcomes your moist humble feet, and soft ancient eyes.

This being the early ruses of May, the dearest child, penitent in
   an orphanage of sunflowers, awakens,

with her rebellious yellow eyes, protected by water and light,
bound meticulously by reef and sand;
she smiles to the ether, and carefully explodes; here we are,
here we go.

Elsewhere, a vine, inconspicuously rises from an aging
ceramic pot, stained army green by the prodigal rains;
she straightens and smiles, unattached, and gleefully
independent.
Just another day, she whispers. Smell that clean country air.

PART 1

A delightfully fresh wind, a perfect curve in the universe.
Burn, burn burn......we are gone.

EPILOGUE:

(The boys amble around, waiting for the tides, trying not to bother anyone,
        perpetually cool and mellow,
           in the late
              morning
                  light).

TIGHT IN ALL THE CLASSY PLACES

*

another fantasy, another breakdown;

the page, riddled with sweethearts and disco balls, all pomp and sweat - tattooed around the hip, tight in all the classy places- butterscotch and rose, milky and shy - talk to you all night, in the groovy silence of being, out at the track.
my hands....nothing but you;
my dreams, nothing but you......Valentines Day cards from the moon, postcards from Saturn's smooth rings.

speaking in venerable tongues, being the air between sand and rock, special, proper, illustrious, shining, deep, subjective, still caring; listening to house music in the late morning, up all night, fresh from Seminyak, DJ Falcone and the party girl surf camp sweethearts;
(and the French dude suddenly wakes up, gets off the couch, and vomits straight into the kitchen sink);
proper foundations of calligraphy, amphetamines and sex shop holograms - stay close to the speaker, turn up the bass, pretty pretty - break out the markers, bomb the local beaches......
(its everything).
"this is what life should be like, but with surfing" he laments;

Lightning Bolts and Disco Girls

and the black girls boogie woogie,
and the dude in a vanilla suit growls into the microphone:
   Daddy Cool........
speak now, be a hero, be a star, be an animal, be wild–
the professional perspective, the funk and castrations, the
   style, the magnificent humming of time (fabulous
   again.....);
she dances and snaps some photos, then dances again, while
   her boyfriend kills it on the turntables, and the whole club
   lunges into the steaming unsecured future;
then the morning light breaks through the late night sky,
   and the hippies all go home, and the lovers forget about it,
   and the hustlers pay up, and the cool kids go to Magdelana,
   and the long boarders are cool again.

no fuk around

every night you are a wet dream, every day you are a needle;
pay them dues, mellow as water, preaching civil disobedience;
we are all free now, we are all love now;
we are all special, beautiful, young forever, eternally gorgeous,
   blissfully broke, with hands raised to the sky, hailing the
   peace, hailing the love;
now go get it! now give me a hug.

all night Danny Teneglia sessions, all day water practice.

UTERLY
USELESS

*

1

"that boy is wicked smart....."
and she looks the same as all the rest;
patience, letters and water.
the alarms go off: what a beautiful.......my darling.......
   my favorite tree, my ego;
tempests and winds, in nature, what you do best:
conceive of victory, of love, of gratitude – what does that look like?
popular opinion dominates the evening news, though i've gone to the bank.
they suggest buying T bills, rolling trucks, and renting Cadillacs – for everyone;
the rich have consumed all the pastrami sandwiches in paradise, a short prayer for the rehab chicks, the yoga school confessionals, the jungle confessionals;
plant me next to the river, wave a hand at the passing strangers,
la
  la
    la
virtuoso hand massages, obligatory small talk –

don't worry about a thing,
you
  are
    doing
      great.
uh oh.......
"fuck your heroes" he says,
and throws a can of tear gas at all those protesters.
Nature is sitting at the local bus stop, sipping on some ginger
  juice and reflecting:

mmmmm, this juice sure is good.
maybe make the sun come up tomorrow.

2

the ambitions are rearing their dirty heads, the life like barbie
  dolls are getting on the first plane out;
the rains have started.......
don't call her unless you plan to fuck her - thats the maxim.
the actors all received free tickets to Paris, the trash is still in
  Jersey; he is such a star! they scream. he is so macho.
poets are pussies; pass the hot sauce;
living next to a palm tree, identical to that rich couple in
  black;
hold my hand, act natural.
plenty of things to do here - much better in the warm sun.
everyday a hashtag revelation,
everyday a new women to say i love you to.
she was up all night, i can tell by reviewing her Facebook
  posts- finally! you have something interesting to say.

now practice.

the bebop decision: mellow bru.

handshakes all around
(at least she is not sleeping with anyone else, yet);
mellow bru – come try this shape;
diesel and pretty, with no one to tell,
of course that chick made a fucking ton of noise last night,
and now she lays on the ground – the king is dead! long live
   the king......
the CBGB's crowd will hate you now;
the waif girls are ordering from the deli counter:
   "a pound of brisket, that salami in the window, and three
   sour pickles, please."
love the body, love the soul,
arrive for some savasana, aware of her curling lips and
   awkward smile;
one ticket for Miami please – on my way to Israel,
the only girl you've ever really loved – the only woman you
   could not love;
was this what Whitman meant by free? is this the urban jet
   lag they warned me of?
poetry of the ego, over that phat base line,
jungle jungle, hold me near.

3

a lovely place to spend the hurricane, a treacherous outing in
   the sun; premium floor seats, missed jump shots and gravy
   – take me home, its utterly useless here....
the rage the rage, a giant backbend,
take this to the valley – "i got your valley right here......"
the trade winds are up, the town is empty and closed for the
   season; shuttered gates and empty tables; the feeling of loss,
   the deep echo of time –
hollow, grateful, bombed out and sunburned – all the dudes
   on the road pass and smile,
dirty and indiscriminate, working full time for that Nobel

Lightning Bolts and Disco Girls

Prize, hammered again on the inside.
special piece of paradise, so silent, the issues of yesterday take
   hold, true peace and love, he says; how long have we been
   watching this burning?
utterly useless, fully aware – on the avenues they want more
   jobs and healthcare,
at home she has less and less to do – age is arriving,
   adulthood is waiting,
in the sleazy shadows, with the bankers and the used car
   salesman;
a word for the press agents, another profitable year down on
   the street, they say;
from the silent movie shoot in Leon to the seaside cafe in
   Marsielle;
it all smells like fish.
where
   did
     you
       get the
         courage?
they pitch you way inside,
they come for your children and seeds.
soil sellers, dope smugglers, anti heroes, abortion rights
   activists and antisemites,
around and around and around – the camera crew is outside,
   here is your packed lunch;
yes, i admit to being self indulged in the world of others,
   stalker for a day,
social hemophiliac, bunting in order to get on base;
but this is the first time anyone has asked me to the
   dance.......
a world away from there, hip and anxious, letting all the cool
   kids play hopscotch on the front lawn;
dinner for two please, and make it snappy.
charmer

UTERLY USELESS

five cent hussy
headstand hustler
pay me the rent money, before she is out on the street again.
all dressed in black, reciting Angela Davis, in time with
  Freddie Hubbard,
up all night with Mahalia Jackson, under the train tracks with
  Brigitte Anne-Marie Bardot;
you are a successful sex symbol, and Oprah is calling
  again......
pay me that candy money, you sly ass motherfucker......
where'd you find him at?
he was stuck in a tree, around uptown Manhattan.

he sings confidently, slowly:
forget your lust, for the rich mans gold; all that you need, is in your
  soul....
treading water with the waif models fresh off the bus, in that
  grim room with terrible lighting, the stench of antiseptic,
the vinegar based diet will keep you trim and tan, he says;
watching the color photos of the raw diet thespians over the
  world wide web;
water! oh water! just a moment to yourself perhaps?
you ask for nothing; you are such a charmer......

motherfucker.......pass the peas.....

fallen hippie, misfit star, jacked up and impersonal,
telling all the young dancing girls they look great.
scheming - burning - pressure, ok...creepy;
yes, you are creepy.
and you dream of her, and you dream of her.

and you dream of her.

Lightning Bolts and Disco Girls

OBEROI
AND DRAGON

*

sashe and beauty - no tricks, no posing.
Dylan went back out on the road to let the tribe know what
was up. 1975. from the Pacific to The Garden. Ginsberg at the
 wheel, Ratso with a pen.

AUM.....(deeply).

the residents get in line, all dressed in white, shackled, waiting
 for the bullets.
don't worry, they hear the dreamers say. this will only hurt for a
 moment......
welcome back lady love machine, weed killer, penniless
 dreamer, American with a backpack.
welcome to the island, now get in line.

the freedom and the expensive juice list.......

mama shanti, and her radical trails of goji berries and space age
 asanas.
gasping for breath, hoarding all the water.
its the water thats gonna get us......

Shiva and the daily prophesy, Einstein and the bicycle. Kuta is
  burning up, got the clap, the shim sham sand dance,
  the Dharamsala head stand hour - free for the killer whale
  lovelies and the hula hoop wake up artists.

don't miss me to much, she commands. might mean
  something important.

special, and her tight grip.
hand shakes with the President and the hit squads, preaching
  her EPMD in the dirt parking lot. who is that? who are
  you?

present, and the courage to be here.
satya grin and the first stop on the bus after El Paso, after
  Altamont, after Manhattan.
from Oakland, he says flatly. people always think Brooklyn,
  but thats the other black guy.....
a harmless mix up, with the gun and the spoken word
  gangsters on stage.
the smile, challenging, but the honeymoon suite is still open.

let them all go.....

miracles on Oberoi, sunsets in the sand.
a jiggle and a ginger twist, puts the tints in color and the
  foam back home.

cool with the vegetarians and Russian models - peace for the
  asana misfits and toxin free heavy weights.
peace and love, he hears again. groovy, with a straight wind
  and a dragon bowl.
a model citizen. makes Gandhi proud.

some days its the chase, some days its the catch.

gorilla tendencies in the pseudo urban sprawl.
avoid the Russian models, The Gods instruct. thats straight
   suicide.

let them all go.

hati hati beauty queen and a wandering vegan saint saunter
   into a small cafe on Oberoi and listen to all the happening
   accents: hipster wedding planners, entrepreneurs and
   backpackers, on a roll with a scarf and a small Yudilele;
   dating the ghost of Tom Wolfe, trickery with the well
   dressed saints and the mad under sexed globe
   trotters.

independent! The Gods yell. put it all into the sand.
buried, heavy and all over the place – anything can happen;
   hiding out in the studios, what TD is doing with all his
   time.
mild mannered and insane – best kind of lovers.
California surprise girls with a long time smile, hearing
   a Sidney lunatic talking the miles, all because she left.

all because she left.....

the sunshine burns through, the Peruvian times and the
   rambling wifi.
been a moonshiner now for many long years, as the man
   said.
caught a train for the coast, hanging in the islands,
   successfully doing less, and breathing well.

never doubt that a small group.....

confined in the prime time, elegant with and without the salt
   water.

Lightning Bolts and Disco Girls

catered the big white party in town, groovy again with the
   money honeys and the real galaxy drop outs.
taken in time, wild around the edges, painting with a lead
   pencil and a French infatuation - sure, they are all
   crazy.......

easy does it. the weirder the better.

she sings a four bar blues riff down by the beach:
don't tell me your name/don't tell me your town/just your
   body/just one night.

the butterflies are everywhere, a new toy and a hungry soul.
peace and love, bartender. peace and love.
with a thin slice of lime and a sugar sugar back.
turn up the radio, my good man..... think they are playing
   The James Brown Hour again.

shanti shanti, hubba hubba.

DEAR OLD
FRIENDS

*

You cant take it with you; all heroically dying; fabulous; in the center of the universe; strange and lovely.
Satvic confessions – the transference – the lack of small talk.
Whom do you feel comfortable with? Whom do you love? Now shut the fuck up.
Infinite and elegant, a stray dog, a wild cowboy; the worn brakes on an old Buick, the new blues in the same old town.
Loose, spellbound and breaking, with all the pretty girls in aisle five;
Shape me something special – wake up with someone new.
Girlfriend, star, lazy half back, giant wave – bound for less ordinary, in ways dangerous and dear;
They may murder for these words, and no one is coming to save you.

(You are a genius, and no one is coming to save you).

And they laugh, bouncing along a dry dirt road, through the indecent jungle, dense and heaving.
Style....it's all about style........;
Wrapped in color, silent and beautiful, praying without the PR, blessed beyond recognition, empty,

Lightning Bolts and Disco Girls

Smelling like sandalwood and peanut butter, banana vinegar juice and 4AM sex talk,
With memories of the silence, her suspecting smile (the roller coaster, the hif fi morning and ex lover pedigrees),
The Iggy Pop tantra affairs, the disco head;
The tour, the deep take off, the love machine
(Don't worry, it's all heavy, it's all just a dream).

Pretty boys and their shiny new blue suede shoes – just taking her for a spin, will be back before sunset......
Just sit there and let them look – its what you get for flying commercial;
Everyone wonders, everyone has a standing room only education;
HI, MY NAME IS BURT RUSSEL – DAMN GOOD TO FINALLY MEET YOU!

she says I'm ok, I'm alright, now that you have gone, from my life; now everything, should be alright.

If you go deep, really, all tough and nonchalant, all dressed in rags and shining like gold, with no plans and no exit strategy, then it might just work.....The Gods are considerate. Paying what you got, paddling out, he took the last train off of Weaver Street, and then suddenly the pension is gone, and the thugs are waiting to lift you over their broad shoulders, and love you some more, for the apricot and pumpkin seed lifestyle, and the ahimsa street corner shape jobs; a true corner hero, a beach God; a damn hunger, a simple plan.

Just don't get Dengue, The Gods whisper; freely admitting a consensual oneness,

When she closes the front door, and leaves for Toronto.

YOUNG GIRL
BLUES

*

Shotgun shacks and lonely nights, Gill Scott Heron playing in
   the background,
White girl monster maker, looking better in leather,
The song changes, suddenly, as he pulls out.

Another generation in the bleacher seats, another third row
   performance.
The whole town is a roller rink, the local chicks put their
   stilettos on backwards;
From side to side, from side to side.
Mess with these blue eyes and you watch how my dagger
   shines.
All your fancy words and Be Bop cool, don't mean a thing
   down here on 4th Street,
Haven't you heard the song?

Damn......

And for those who hear the music – and for those sentimental
   piercings, she is up late, online, posting inspirational videos
   and wallpaper quotes, sipping white wine alone from a dirty
   plastic cup, with the reverends all waiting outside the gates,

Lightning Bolts and Disco Girls

barefoot and chubby in the sun - nothing as beautiful.
Take a deep breath, sigh; resigned to local foreplay and
   international business;
It's never too late, it's never the cash - if they stop fighting
   for a moment, if he manages to make it through the night,
   if you hold onto that dream and cut out the noise, then
   the Rockettes might get your shiver, the Pope may swing
   through for tea;
A massive coronary, tells you to eat chocolate cake for
   breakfast, to leave love at the door,
As if no one dares; and everyone silently creeps away when
   you get ill, yet speak so highly of you online.
What a grand gesture!
What a young girl phenomenon!
Blessed, and answering telephones for the National
   Government, uncompromising in your dedication to Shiva;
make it one for my baby/and one more for the road.

The numbers came out today - we are still broke.......;
Its still wonderful.
Show them the new summer styles, while I lounge here and
   act important;
While the fratricide of BUSY hails a cab and goes uptown;
While the big shot hipsters lull around the beach entrance
   and look perfect;
While the cotton candy prices go up, and the coconut oil is
   free on the corner.
(another pizza for my young friend please; another mango
   for the fat kid).
So beautiful and anxious in the mid day sun;
Winding through the empty streets of Sicily, actively looking
   for trouble.
Standing around empty, waiting for one of the girls to give
   you a kiss.
The James Dean look alike contest in blue, the Natalie

YOUNG GIRL BLUES

Portman genocide in red;
Where my girl at?
Basement tapes and dime store hussies, Buddha blow jobs
   and left over tabs of acid.
It takes a lot to be a hero; it takes one morning to be a star.
Put it over there by the slave ships,
Be sure to leave a tip for the long shore man.
Everybody loves you – everybody is dancing.

We've just returned from Ghana,
We've just bought court side tickets for the Knicks;
Empty and blessed, drunk and holy;
Over here! Over here! you say – tang tops and faded blue
   jeans for everybody!
Examine the intention, let go of the story;
Free and mighty, free and clear – a longing for the abstract
   berated verse of love,
A trip around the world for a dream and a cup of water;
Don't say anymore, don't ruin the honesty –
fiending for money and alcohol/the life of a West Side;
Don't worry, they will all find you eventually.

Watching the ocean from a seat in the soft sand, speaking
   about romance and youth,
While the older men peer in through the curtain, and
   promise to make you happy.
Healthy, skinny, shinning bright, freshly tan, smiling; just back
   from the coast.......just another girl....
There is nothing new on the message board today, there are
   no emails pretending to hurt;
The aches, the infections, the words.
Of course I want to fuck you, he says. I'm a man, not a
   eugenic.
You retreat further into desperation, and reveal dreams to the
   other heartbreak angels

Posing for another smokey photo, taken by a bemused
   stranger who promises love;
There is a light where the heart used to be, a runway where
   the brain once lay;
Bohemian death star, a lovely mess; push through and want
   nothing in return.

The fabulous weight of simple living wraps an arm around
   your neck and welcomes you in.
peace to the Gods/peace to the earth.....
21st century misfit, dancing queen, ruby midnight eyes and
   those Madonna curves;
Turn the lights off, come sit over here......
The taste of gasoline, the late night resistance – you put up
   such a fight for a poor girl;
Straighten out those bangs, lend me a quarter (just slide it
   into the slot).
Manic jungle parades, lifetime achievement awards
   premature,
The local Tica laureate, the last ring on the heartbreak ladder;
Wild, transcending, a simple atom bomb explosion inside the
   chest, in an empty room,
At a reserved table, on a longboard, on top of an elephant –
   pandering, you have successfully ruined your chances, you
   have been indentured into service (finally!)
The echoes of conceit plead guilty to a misfired romance, an
   easy screw, a real doozy;
And still the operators put me on hold.
This is Richard Nixon calling, do you have anymore Bobby
   Dylan LP,s?

The peppery tones of age and insolence rattle around an
   empty room;
All the leggy punk models and out of work strippers are
   sauntering through the hotel lobby,

YOUNG GIRL BLUES

Painfully waiting for a quick view of George Clooney and
 his merry gang of celebritants.
With such gusto! With such bust!
International daily monologues and pangs of brilliance litter
 the same wasteland as tech start ups and young American
 poetry,
Says *peace to the Gods, peace to the earth.......*
It's your place or mine sweetheart – flip a coin and hold my
 hand – the interest is waning.......
Yet still we are so lucky, and the hurtful pangs of gratitude
 litter the open road;
From this tiny peephole in the earth to that grand center in
 the sky – awake!
And all the boys persist in loving you greatly.

Secretly it's a mess, a dire heartbreak, a lethargic aha moment;
Young girl in rags, again, colorful as the sky, deep as the
 ocean, lending perspective, selling karma tickets and
 watching pro basketball; announcing your plans for travel
 and money,
Escaping the glue of mediocrity (you hope)
For the European coasts, the jet set sun life elsewhere,
Where the drinks are stronger and the men are wealthier.
Cringing at the ceremonial lust crusades through Hells
 Kitchen, sampling the latest fare at the most expensive
 fusion restaurants in South America;
Continuously bold and beautiful – a merchant sits on the
 front steps and waits for the lunch crowd
(the healthy callings of sun colored carrot juice and the
 grinding revolution of happy blenders),
Piercing the night sky, lost in another black and white dream
– Illustrious, broke, happy, free – parading around the upscale
 parking lots in song;
A luminous smile, a new theory for relativity ($E = DE + X$),
 a pandering slow song that no one will ever hear,

Lightning Bolts and Disco Girls

Breakdowns and preachers outside the neighborhood
   laundry mats;
We are all in it together, you say.
Pass the peas, they reply.
"Be bold, and great forces will come to your aid" she recites;
So you remain standing on the bridge, and watch the traffic
   pass.
Mentally fertile and physically brave, slashing tires along
   Rodeo Drive, figuring out the combination to the padlock
   on the beach;
Emotionally drained, the fatigue at watching another failed
   lover pass, at viewing the weight of gold increase with
   every hungry day (and still so hungry?);
Manhandled and delightful, radiant along the muddy banks
   of the river Seine,
Presenting the best dressed award to the punk and blues
   artists who tag up the museums;
How rich and extroverted, how coarse and perfect – in the
   morning stillness with the heavy burden of silence,
Breathing (as the angels do), preferring the back of the bus,
   contracting out the hard labour to friends and family,
Leaving a generous donation upon the thirsty flower beds
   and hungry wishing wells;
The darkness is passing, you surmise – the temples are calling;
A grand life filled with laughter and kisses – the heroic
   blends of poetry and business,
The microscopic beginning of it all – the first time he took
   you out dancing;
Should have done more, could have afforded less.......
Make believe debutants and long orange frock coats arrive
   from the first world – it's a disaster, it's a party now.

And for those who hear the music – careening around empty
   street corners on new years day, picking fights with weary
   city bouncers, adding jive and spice to the list of ghetto

YOUNG GIRL BLUES

prerequisites (what options do you really have?);
Successfully killing the dream, ultimately talking about
 yourself:
Make me smarter! she howls.
Make me whole.

Regressions – a supreme shot to the head under a clear blue
 sky, holding an expired passport,
Going fast and fast and fast;
Water! the dream, the process.
The illusions are clear and affordable, the dating game is
 infinite.

She has left for the mountains, she has swiftly chosen
 anonymity;
A break in the chain, a little Sam Cooke to end a romance.
Goodnight little river, goodnight sweat song.

Dirty, believe it.

Lightning Bolts and Disco Girls

OF ROME
AND
SINGAPOUR

*

That same shallow water refuge, those indelible Mandela words:
   cutting, sharply cutting.......
As a small boy, a restless child, a delinquent, unfolded, here,
   the same as stardust, the pesky enduring white woman
   hunger; arresting, solitary, the passing protocols of pleasantries,
   destitution, bewilderment; hi, nice to see you again.

Here we are, the townsmen haughtily say; just a fancy track
   of failed escapism and blatant materialism, to chicly delve out,
   accordingly, for all the heavy Jews and skinny waterside girls.

It's a beautiful airport, it's a lovely beach.

The sun enters, purposely, her golden rays and psychotic
   embrace, shimmies past the hungry velvet ropes, the fading
   red carpets – sheltering, real cool;

*Where ever in the world you are, however it all ends up, there is little
fault in these decisive stars, in this lyrical gyration, in this longing
hunger for transcendental silence, touch, and uncensored elegy's on
freedom and Bobby Mcgee.*

Lightning Bolts and Disco Girls

Taken: from the sheets of improvement, youth, inspiration –
the dark clouds swing their weighty polished black batons
at the little red Buddhists gathered outside the steep
embassy steps, neatly arranged at the rainbows crashing
end; and the clouds gaze fundamentally hard, with curled
milk eyes and shattered dream lips; (remorseful), with
shields and bitter instruction manuals – here we go, they
lazily announce – but we gypsies know little else, you
honestly plead; just an indiscriminate wrinkled handful of
sand, you reveal, and a cold river to anxiously wade across

(Joe and his alligators, Slash and his fans)

Fall in love with a dirty Hollywood groupie, he hastily
scribbles in orange spray paint; thick bubbly letters,
hopeful, across the Venice Beach Recreation Area concrete
wall – a final truce, a goodbye note; write a blank check to
diligence, the chorus elders doth protest.

The grass is horribly overgrown, he suddenly realizes; the
temperaments are momentarily failing; even though she
promised a full night out, a long indelible kiss, a spicy
remedy for a pounding loneliness, and swift gliding
shadows; even though her face is shiny coin and her
hips are sharp reef: tantalizing, final selection, she avoided
Buchenwald and Auschwitz, for this seminal three day
grace period, and a fanatical clinging to the awkward left
(and wet!);
thank you for the good times, he whispers, into her smooth
belly.

You are being awkward, she whispers back.
Come around angel, the woes are just that......

She looks sad, branded, with all the long passing faces of

OF ROME AND SINGAPOUR

Rome and Singapore.

we could have gone downtown, he tells her, to the Korean
   bath houses, anytime after midnight, and been cleansed of
   all this money; or the Santa Monica flack jacket reviews,
   with the trendy DJ fashionistas and celebrity time zone
   freelance artists: that would have been fun......

We could have traveled together, upon the same pin stripped
   zoot suit kite, without the boring complaints of designer
   luggage and religious mercy; you, perched heartily upon
   one silver wing, and myself dangling from the sides of a
   dusty Mack truck, watching you get famously higher, with
   the Brooklyn bartender girls, and the Battery Park lepers,
   in bright daring colors, never going home again.

We could have persisted, in the fading rotten California
   light, with an upper middle class family and dim prospects,
   under a black tarp, feeling ourselves temporarily clean and
   permanently voluptuous, kicking up the coast along
   highway number one, promising the obedient stars that this
   is the last affair, the beginning of something great:
a Broadway review, a popular song; past the gay harps and
   jagged rocks, attempting to catch the color of night in
   poem and bottle, never again considered alone, or envious.

The candle light is perfect, you say. The vegetables are just
   right.

(They light a fire, in a tall rotund clay pot, hauled over
   asphalt, in the back of a rusty blue Chevy, from the South
   Western dessert plains, it sits perfectly, within a clean round
   hand made black metal stand.
Then *they* scurry away, with hasty orders from Atlas: another
   chromosome to split, clean, straight down the middle, for

Africa, and her wandering children) .

Drenched, in limelight and thyme, fickle for a cause,
convinced of a cosmic revolution, her inherent seductive
imperfections – the first days light, peaceful, eagerly greets
the roving cataclysmic garbage men, teetering on the edge
of sketched genius, dusting off their fabled Nobel Prizes.

The cities insane taxi driver pugilists pull up to Wall Street
and empty their shallow pockets – the ceremonial spilling
of lonely coins for a troubled middle-aged capitalist, the
continual jungle tremors call him weak;
we have nothing to say! a young boy wails, and sketches a
clean unified theory across the Gestapo bathroom walls.

This day, labeled like no other, casts a heavy veil of
permanence, confidently draped over the shoulders of
youthful ambitions, of steadily aging judgements: come
here young elephant, remember the moss strew path, with
the slippery rocks, and thin ripples of water passing around
their tiny bulk; just her wandering sad melodies to keep
you warm, never far from the garden, always harassed by
the universe, and her mischievous doings; you could have
been anything, the sky carelessly whispers, smiling greatly
upon her wet kings, her lazy chosen bunch, her roving
Krishna delinquents.
Your dreams are answered, the sky bellows; no way back now.

*She poses nude next to the beach, watches the headlines with great
interest, then gets back on the bus, and quietly drives away.*

Have you heard of my death? he asks her softly; its been
highly anticipated.

OF ROME AND SINGAPOUR

Lightning Bolts And **Disco Girls**

About the Author

Douglas Evan Weiss was born and raised
in New York City.
He is the author of *Killer Mario Cuomo,
Junglehead, Cobras And Caviar*, and *Surfhead*.
He currently resides between Costa Rica and Bali.
He is forever grateful to his friends and family
for a lifetime of support and encouragement..

www.ingramcontent.com/pod-product-compliance
Lightning Source LLC
Chambersburg PA
CBHW051352290426
44108CB00015B/1987